Third Edition.

Revised to January, 1916.

THE

OFFICIAL REGULATIONS

FOR

VOLUNTEER TRAINING

CORPS

AND FOR

COUNTY VOLUNTEER

ORGANISATIONS

(ENGLAND AND WALES.)

EDITED BY J. P. BLAKE.

The Naval & Military Press Ltd

Published by

The Naval & Military Press Ltd

Unit 5 Riverside, Brambleside
Bellbrook Industrial Estate
Uckfield, East Sussex
TN22 1QQ England

Tel: +44 (0)1825 749494

www.naval-military-press.com
www.nmarchive.com

*In reprinting in facsimile from the original, any imperfections are inevitably reproduced
and the quality may fall short of modern type and cartographic standards.*

GENERAL CONTENTS.

(FOR DETAILS SEE INDEX AT END.)

References in all cases refer to paragraphs (which are in black figures) and not to pages.

CONTENTS—*continued.*

COVERING NOTE.

The Rules and Regulations for Volunteer Training Corps contained in this volume are issued by the Central Association for the direction and instruction of all ranks; they embrace, and in some cases amend, all the orders and decisions circulated up to this date. From the date of their publication every Volunteer will be bound by the Regulations contained herein, and it will be assumed, as is the regulation in the Army, that all are familiar with their terms; ignorance of regulations is no excuse for their breach.

Reference will be by paragraph, and the number will be quoted in any order issuing from the Central Association.

Volunteers are expected to loyally accept these Regulations, and to carry them out in accordance with the best traditions of His Majesty's Army.

O'MOORE CREAGH,
General.
Military Adviser, C.A.V.T.C.

January, 1916.

SECTION I.

AUTHORITY AND RECOGNITION.

SECTION I.

AUTHORITY AND RECOGNITION.

PARA.

1. Lord Desborough (President, C.A.V.T.C.) received the following letter in acknowledgment of the report he forwarded to His Majesty the King on the progress of the Volunteer Training scheme:—

H.M. the King and the Volunteer Corps.

"Royal Pavilion, Aldershot Camp.

My dear DESBOROUGH,—The King desires me to thank you for your letter of the 8th instant. He is delighted to read your satisfactory report of the progress of the Volunteer Training scheme.

No doubt these battalions will be very useful in assisting the National Reserve in such work as guarding bridges and lines of communication. Indeed, the instances you give show how much they are already in request. His Majesty is only too glad to think that anything he has been able to do may have helped on the movement.—Yours very truly,

21*st March*, 1915.   (*Signed*)   STAMFORDHAM."

The following is an extract from a speech by the Prime Minister in the House of Commons relative to the Volunteer movement:—

Prime Minister on Volunteer Training Corps.

2. "The Central Association Volunteer Training "Corps, which has taken up this matter in a "thoroughly practical manner, has been recognised by "the Government for this purpose. Local bodies should "affiliate themselves to it—which may be done without "charge—in order that suitable assistance and super- "vision may be given to local efforts of this nature."

17*th November*, 1914.

WAR OFFICE, *12th April*, 1915.

3. Dear Mr. HARRIS,—I am writing to acknowledge your letter of the 12th April, and the receipt of the set of papers and forms issued from the Central Association.

I would take this opportunity of expressing our appreciation of the work which you and the Central Association are doing in organising the Volunteer movement in accordance with the principles laid down by the War Office.

In taking over this work, the Association has not only considerably lightened the burdens of the War Office, but, I feel sure, it is proving a valuable ally to our Recruiting Organisation.—Believe me, yours sincerely,

(Signed) H. SCLATER,

Adjutant-General.

Officers.

4. OFFICERS OF THE CENTRAL ASSOCIATION.

President.
The Lord Desborough, K.C.V.O.

Military Adviser.
General Sir O'Moore Creagh, V.C., G.C.B., G.C.S.I.

Hon. Treasurer.
C. J. Stewart (The Public Trustee).

Hon. Secretary.
Percy A. Harris, L.C.C.

Assistant Secretary.
W. Graham Everitt.

Vice-Presidents.

The Duke of Norfolk, K.G., G.C.V.O.; The Duke of Rutland; The Duke of Portland, K.G., G.C.V.O.; The Marquess of Lincolnshire, K.G.; The Earl of Essex; The Earl of Coventry; The Earl of Jersey, Earl Brownlow; The Earl of Dartmouth; The Earl Waldegrave; The Earl of Warwick; The Earl of Mount-Edgcumbe, G.C.V.O.; The Earl of Craven; The Earl of Lonsdale; The Earl of Harewood, K.C.V.O.; The Earl Beauchamp, K.G.,

K.C.M.G.; The Earl of Dunraven, K.P., C.M.G.; The Earl of Leicester, G.C.V.O., C.M.G.; The Earl of Plymouth; The Lord Harris, G.C.S.I., G.C.I.E.; Major-General The Lord Cheylesmore, K.C.V.O.; The Lord Nunburnholme, D.S.O.; Major-General The Lord Ranksborough, C.V.O., C.B.; The Lord Muir Mackenzie, G.C.B.; The Lord Mayor of London; Admiral Lord Charles Beresford, G.C.B., M.P.; Sir John Cotterell, Bart.; Sir Hugh Bell, Bart.; Sir Herbert Mackworth Praed, Bart.; Sir T. Courtenay Warner, Bart., C.B., M.P.; The Hon. H. Cubitt, C.B.; The Hon. Mr. Justice Scrutton; Sir Henry Craik, K.C.B., M.P.; Sir Godfrey Lagden, K.C.M.G.; Sir Arthur Conan Doyle; Solomon J. Solomon, Esq., R.A.; J. E. Greaves, Esq.; G. A. Bonner, Esq.; T. A. Edge, Esq.; L. St. Loe Strachey, Esq.

Executive Committee.

The Lord Desborough, K.C.V.O.; General Sir O'Moore Creagh, V.C., G.C.B., G.C.S.I.; C. J. Stewart; Percy A. Harris, L.C.C.; G. A. Bonner (Legal Adviser).

Military Committee.

General Sir O'Moore Creagh, V.C., G.C.B., G.C.S.I.; Lieut.-General Sir Henry Settle, K.C.B., D.S.O.; Major-General D. C. F. Macintyre, C.B.; Brigadier-General Abbott, C.B.; Colonel W. B. Creagh; Colonel Ridgeway, V.C., C.B.; Colonel Brooke Taylor; Major Bartlett, V.D.; Arthur Head (Hon. Secretary).

Finance Committee.

The Lord Desborough, K.C.V.O.; C. J. Stewart; F. Warner; John Boraston; J. H. Seaverns; E. W. Giffard; B. Hansford, C.B.; H. Batty-Smith.

5.

20
Gen. No.
3604
(A G.I.)

WAR OFFICE, LONDON, S.W.,

7*th April*, 1915.

Letter to Lord
Desborough,
K.C.V.O.,
from the
Army Council
recognising
the Executive
Committee.
MY LORD,

Owing to the large development of the business and work of the Central Association Volunteer Training Corps, to which recognition was granted under certain conditions by War Office letter No. 20/General Number/ 3604 (A.G.I.) of the 19th November, 1914, I am commanded to inform you that the Army Council consider it desirable for the sake of convenience to vest certain powers in the hands of a limited number of officials of the Association as an Executive Committee.

I am therefore to inform you that the approval of the Council is given for the formation of such an Executive Committee, composed of the following members of your Association : —

Yourself,

General Sir O'Moore Creagh, V.C., G.C.B., G.C.S.I.,

Mr. C. J. Stewart,

Mr. Percy A. Harris.

The function of this Committee will be that of affiliating Volunteer Corps to the Central Association and of acting as a recognised channel of communication between the War Office and affiliated Volunteer Corps.

I am,

Sir,

Your obedient servant,

(Signed) B. B. CUBITT.

The Rt. Hon. Lord Desborough, K.C.V.O.,
President, Central Association Volunteer Training Corps, London, W.C.

6. OBJECTS OF THE CENTRAL ASSOCIATION.

1. To assist recruiting for the Regular and Territorial Army.

Objects of the Association.

2. To encourage men not of age for service in the Regular Forces, or, if of age for Service, who have a genuine reason for not joining the Regular Army (in the latter case they must sign the form of undertaking mentioned in the War Office letter to Lord Desborough, dated the 19th November, 1914, see below), to form themselves into Volunteer Corps in order to learn, in their spare time, the elements of military drill, and rifle shooting.

3. To organise the various Volunteer Corps throughout the country into Battalions and Regiments, taking as the geographical basis of such Organisation the County area; to provide Rules and Regulations for such Volunteer Corps; to secure their military efficiency; to act as a connecting link between them and the War Office and to enforce such Regulations as the War Office may issue.

7. CONDITIONS OF RECOGNITION.

20

Gen. No.

3604

(A.G.I.)

WAR OFFICE, LONDON, S.W.,

19th November, 1914.

My LORD,—In confirmation of the arrangements made with you in various interviews, I am commanded to inform you that the Army Council are prepared to grant recognition to the Central Association Volunteer Training Corps, as long as a responsible officer approved by the War Office is its adviser, and the Council will extend that recognition to such Volunteer Forces and Rifle Clubs, etc., as may become affiliated to your Association, and decide to abide by your rules.

Army Council Letter of Recognition.

The following rules have been framed as the conditions under which the Army Council are prepared to grant recognition to your Association, and to those which may be affiliated thereto : —

1. It is to be clearly understood that only the names of those can be registered who are not eligible through age to serve in the Regular or Territorial Army, or are unable to do so for some genuine reason which is to be recorded in the Corps Register; in the case of the latter, they must agree in writing to enlist if specially called upon to do so.

2. No arms, ammunition or clothing will be supplied from public sources, nor will financial assistance be given.

3. There may be uniformity of dress among members of individual organisations provided that no badges of rank are worn, and provided that the dress is distinguishable from that of Regular and Territorial Units.

4. Members of recognised organisations will be allowed to wear as a distinctive badge a red armlet of a breadth of three* inches with the letters G. R. inscribed thereon. The badge will be worn on the left arm above the elbow.

5. The accepted military ranks and titles will not be used or recognised, and no uniform is to be worn except when necessary for training.

6. No form of attestation involving an oath is permitted.

7. It will be open to Army Recruiting Officers to visit the Corps at any time and to recruit any members found eligible for service with the Regular Army whose presence in the Corps is not accounted for by some good and sufficient reason.

A circular letter, of which a copy is attached, is being sent to all those corps which have applied to the War Office on various questions dealing with their formation.

I am, My Lord,

Your Lordship's obedient Servant,

R. N. Brade.

---

* Since altered to five,

15

8. Copy of a letter sent by the War Office in reply to two inquiries from Volunteer Corps in reference to Clauses 1 and 7 of the War Office letter to Lord Desborough, dated 19th of November last, Reference 20/Gen.No./3604, (A.G.I.).

Army Council Interpretation of Clauses One and Seven of War Office Letter 20/Gen. No./3604 (A.G.I.). 20/3/15.

"Sir,—I am commanded by the Army Council to acknowledge the receipt of your letter, undated, and in reply to the questions contained therein to inform you that men of military age who join a Volunteer Corps are asked to sign an undertaking to join the Army if specially called upon to do so, in order to show that they are not using the Volunteer Movement in order to shirk the greater responsibilities. This undertaking is not a mere formality, and a man signing it is expected to fulfil his obligation. If a man who may be called upon is not in a position to fulfil his engagement, he can leave the Corps.

"I am to refer you to the following extract from Mr. Tennant's speech in the House of Commons on Monday, 1st instant:—

'In cases where good and sufficient reasons are not shown, a man ought not to be allowed to take the lesser obligation when he ought to fulfil the greater obligation of serving with the Colours. The Hon. Gentleman asked what power we have. We can only use the power of persuasion, but, at all events, I do not think that the Hon. Gentleman need have any alarm that these passages to which he refers in the Document, contain anything in the nature of Conscription. I should like to relieve the House of any apprehension that they may have on that Subject by informing them that all possible powers of persuasion are being used. I would add how greatly we appreciate this great self-sacrifice of the men who are joining these Corps.'

I am,
Sir,
Your obedient Servant,
(Signed)   B. B. CUBITT."

9. Copy of a letter sent to the Central Association of Volunteer Training Corps from the War Office dealing with the position of Railwaymen:—

Railwaymen (A.G.I.).

" Sir,

In reply to yours of the 13th instant, I am directed to say that we cannot allow any alteration in the form of undertaking, but as there is at present an understanding with Railway Companies that men shall only be enlisted with their consent, this will be held to be operative, while it lasts, when questions of enlistment from the ranks of a Volunteer force come up.

I am,
Sir,
Your obedient Servant,
(Signed)   H. R. VAUGHAN, Colonel."

20th March, 1915.

10. In reference to the definition of the words "genuine reason" for men of military age, there has been no interpretation of these words by the War Office. The Central Association, however, has laid down three classes of cases that can be taken as definite:—

Clause I.
War Office
Letter,
19/11/14.
Definition
of Genuine
Reason.

C.A.V.T.C.,
8/2/15,
Form XXI.

(*a*) Government Contracts. These include not only work on arms and ammunition, but Government contracts for boots, clothing, etc. (It has been laid down by the Home Office that men employed on railways have a genuine reason, if they cannot be spared by the Railway Companies.)

(*b*) Government and Municipal employment, such as Clerks in the Admiralty, Inland Revenue, Water Supply, Teachers, where permission to enlist is refused by the Authorities.

(*c*) Physical disabilities, which would include men who have been rejected from the Army by the Medical Officers.

The fourth class are undefined, but should be taken to include cases where enlistment would entail a serious dislocation of business and the throwing of men out of employment. In the case of this last class the Central Association advises the responsible Officer of the Corps to get into communication in the London recruiting area with the Chief Recruiting Staff Officer, and outside that area with the Chief Inspector of Recruiting. All Corps are recommended to invite this Officer to inspect their Corps Register.

Membership of a Volunteer Training Corps neither decreases nor increases a man's obligation to join the Army except in so far as a Corps is visited by a Recruiting Officer and a man is asked to fulfil his obligation as required by War Office letter of the 19th November, 1914. C.A.V.T.C., LII., Nov., 1915.

11. It must be clearly understood that no alteration, or addition, is permissible to paragraph 7 of the Corps Register Form (see Appendix No. 1). This is the clause in which members who have not attained the age of 41, accept the terms of the Army Council letter 19/11/14 (Para. 7). It must be accepted, without qualification of any kind. Men who have completed their military service, and have not attained the age of 46, must also sign this paragraph (see also para. 63 (Military Age)). Army Council Letter must be accepted.

12. " The Secretary of State for War will not agree " to the undertaking to enlist being dependent upon " the leave of Department. The War Office is encourag- " ing those employees who can be spared or for whom " substitutes can be found to enlist in the Regular " Forces. As regards those whose services cannot be " spared, but who have joined Volunteer Training Civil Servants. War Office, 13/4/15

" Corps, recruiting Officers are required to treat such
" cases with every consideration, but the War Office
" cannot give any guarantee not to call upon them to
" enlist, nor can it approve their joining V.T.C. on the
" condition that they will only enlist subject to depart-
" mental approval."

THE HOME OFFICE ON GOVERNMENT POLICY.

Extract from Supplementary Instructions E. to certain Lord-Lieutenants from Home Office, dated 30/11/14.

13. " The policy of the Government is to encourage every man to take his part in the present struggle.

" If he is of proper age and physique, and not excluded from enlistment by employment in Armament Works, Railways, &c., he should enlist.

" If he is not of proper age and physique he should join the nearest Volunteer Corps which is affiliated to the Central Association of Volunteer Training Corps. The War Office have recognised this Association and Volunteer Corps affiliated thereto.

" Every man who takes this latter course will be provided with a Badge and will be counted as a combatant, though no arms, ammunition, or clothing (other than the Badge) will be supplied from Public sources, and no financial assistance will be given.

" Anyone who declines either to enlist or to join an affiliated Volunteer Corps should be informed that he must not take part as a combatant in the defence of his country, and in the case of invasion must be prepared to surrender any arms which he may have in his possession.

" He will be liable to all non-combatant duties, such as digging trenches, burying the dead, &c."

SECTION II.

FORMATION AND CONTROL OF UNITS.

SECTION II.

FORMATION AND CONTROL OF UNITS.

FORMING A CORPS.

14. In the formation of a Volunteer Training Corps, the first step is to appoint a provisional local Committee. If there is a County Association this Committee should communicate with the Regimental Commandant, and request his assistance and co-operation. Only in the event of there being no County Association should the Central Association be communicated with direct. The Committee should approach the Mayor or the Chairman of the District or Parish Council, and request him to summon a meeting of the inhabitants for the purpose of forming a Corps for the town or district. In nearly every case the local authorities have gladly assisted in this Movement for the Defence of the Realm. The Central Association, with the approval of the County Organisation, will arrange to send one of its Honorary Official Speakers to explain the objects and aims of the Association, making no charge beyond the necessary travelling expenses, etc. At this meeting, after a resolution approving of the formation of a Corps has been carried, an Organising Committee should be appointed, and as many men as possible enrolled at once.

It is the task of the Committee to raise the funds necessary for the organisation and equipment of the Corps. The Committee should secure—

    (a) the use of a local school or other public building for drill;

(b) the use of a park or sports field for open-air drill;

(c) a miniature rifle range;

(d) the services of a drill instructor.

In counties where there is a County Association the Officer Commanding must be appointed subject to confirmation by the Regimental Commandant; but in counties where there is no County Association the Officer is appointed locally, subject to the approval of the Central Association.

The same principle applies to affiliation, the issue of the Brassard, and inspection. If there is a County Association, application must be made to the Regimental Commandant; if not, to the Central Association direct. The County Association or Central Association will supply information and a single set of papers free of charge. If required in larger quantities the charge for leaflets is 2s. per hundred (including loose enrolment forms). Enrolment forms are also provided in books, containing a hundred forms, at 2s. 6d. per book, or in lots of fifty books, at 1s. 9d. The Central Association has drawn up and issued the following suggested rules for the use of corps, which it would be well to adopt as far as practicable:—

RULES OF AFFILIATED VOLUNTEER
TRAINING CORPS.

15. 1. That a Volunteer Training Corps, known as the ...., be affiliated to, and accept the Rules of, the Central Association of Volunteer Training Corps; and that there be a Committee of ....; and that (the Mayor of the Borough) or (the Chairman of the Urban District Council) be *ex officio* President of such Committee.

2. That the primary duty of the Corps shall be to promote recruiting for the Regular Army. Only such

men shall be accepted as Members of Volunteer Training Corps who are over military age, or who, if of military age, have a genuine reason for not joining the Regular Army. In the latter case they must sign the undertaking required by the War Office.

3. The first duty of the Committee shall be to appoint a competent Officer to be responsible for the training of the Corps (where there is a County Organisation such appointment shall be subject to the confirmation of the Regimental Commandant). Preliminary training shall be confined to the elements of drill as explained in "Infantry Training, 1914," published by Messrs. Wymans, Limited, of Fetter Lane, E.C., price 6d.

4. All serviceable Rifles or Ammunition in use by the Corps shall be kept at an Armoury, or at some approved place of safe custody. For drill purposes dummy or discarded rifles can be used.

5. For the teaching of rifle shooting arrangements shall be made for the use of a Miniature Rifle Range, which shall only be used while under the control and supervision of a qualified Officer.

6. All men joining the .... Corps shall undertake to remain Members of the Corps until the end of the War, and endeavour to make themselves efficient in drill and rifle shooting and shall maintain the same spirit of military discipline as prevails in His Majesty's Forces. Forty drills of one hour each, and proficiency as a Second-Class Shot entitles a man to the Central Association of Volunteer Training Corps' Proficiency Badge. Ex-Regulars or Ex-Territorials become entitled to these Proficiency Badges on production of a certificate from the Commandant of the Corps to the effect that their general Military knowledge in Drill and Shooting is satisfactory. A member who does not attend a minimum of four drills a month shall be liable to be struck off the roll of the Corps unless absent on leave given by the Commanding Officer of his unit.

7. A Register shall be kept at the Headquarters of the Corps giving age, occupation and previous military experience of each Member of the Corps: where he is of military age the " genuine " reason for not joining the Regular Forces must be clearly stated in the Register, and an undertaking must be placed in the Register by the Member, signed by him, showing that he accepts the terms of the War Office letter, dated 19th November, 1914 (20/Gen. No./3604 " A.G.I.") (see Para. 7). (A Corps Register can be purchased from the Central Association of Volunteer Training Corps at the rate of 1s. 9d. for a book of 50, and 2s. 6d. for a book of 100.)

8. As soon as the Corps is properly constituted an application shall be made to the Central Association of Volunteer Training Corps for the War Office Brassard. (N.B.—Where there is a County Organisation such application should come through the County Organisation; where there is no such Organisation such application should be endorsed by any of the following:—Lord-Lieutenant of the County, Lord Mayor (or Mayor) of Town, Chief Recruiting Officer, Chief Constable, Officer in Command of the District, or, The Central Association Visiting Officer. The Brassard shall always be worn with Uniform; and, when Uniform is not available, it shall always be worn on Parade, or on duty. All Brassards shall be numbered and the name of the wearer indelibly written inside. On a Member ceasing to belong to a Corps he shall return the Brassard to Headquarters, where it shall be destroyed.

9. On the first of each month the Commanding Officer shall send to the Central Association of Volunteer Training Corps a record of the work done by the Corps for the month on the Form provided by the Central Association of Volunteer Training Corps (Form XI.). (Where there is a County Organisation Quarterly Reports must be sent in duplicate by Battalion Commandants to the County Adjutant. See Appendix 7.)

10. Uniform shall not be obligatory, but where adopted shall be of a county pattern (where there is a County Organisation), and shall conform to the Regulations laid down by the Central Association of Volunteer Training Corps (Form XVI., Para. 85). Uniform shall not be worn except on Parade, or on duty.

11. The Committee of a Corps shall appoint a Treasurer who shall be responsible for the funds of the Corps. Members of the Corps will be expected to pay a minimum subscription of ...., which is to be paid into the funds of the Corps. The Committee of the Corps shall be charged with the duty of collecting the funds required for the equipment and organisation of the Corps, but expenditure on the Corps shall only be incurred on the advice of the Officer in command of the Corps. The Committee must in no way interfere with duly appointed officers responsible for the drill, discipline and training.

12. Where there is a County Organisation representing the Central Association the Corps shall link up with the County Regiment and form a platoon, company or battalion of the Regiment, according to its numbers, and recognise the authority of the County Regimental Commandant.

16. The word " Volunteer " is used in Section 1, chapter 1, in the annex to the Hague Convention, as follows:—" In countries where Militia or Volunteer Corps constitute the Army, or form part of it, they are included under the denomination ' Army.' " The word " Volunteer " must therefore be inserted in the titles of all affiliated Corps. *Titles of Affiliated Corps.*

To entitle a man to the status of a belligerent it is necessary that he should belong to a Force recognised by the State. In all official documents issued by the Government this Force is designated by the word " Volunteer." (See also Para. 130.)

Constitution. **17.** The Constitution of all County Regiments must be submitted to the C.A.V.T.C. for approval. In Counties where there is no County Regiment and a Volunteer Corps has a Constitution, such Constitution must also be submitted for approval to the C.A.V.T.C.

County Area. **18.** The Central Association has decided to follow the county area in its organisation of Corps into Battalions and Regiments. The County Organisation, when formed, is the body in each County through whom the Central Association works, and all communications to Corps from the Central Association pass through the County Headquarters.

Affiliation. **19.** Corps or detachments desiring to be affiliated to the Central Association must apply for affiliation to the Regimental Commandant where there is a County Regiment, and where there is not to the Hon. Secretary, Central Association. Affiliation is provisional, and is not complete until the Corps is inspected and passed by an accredited inspecting Officer.

New Corps. **20.** Where a Corps or detachment affiliated to the C.A.V.T.C. already exists in a locality, no new Corps should be started there without the approval of the Regimental Commandant, and where no County Regiment exists, without the approval of the Central Association.

County Affiliation

C.A.V.T.C. XXXVI., 26/7/15, Form XV.

21. Where a County Regiment exists the Central Association dispenses with the separate affiliation of each of its detachments with the Central Association. As the War Office looks to the Central Association for a record of where all Volunteers are located, it is necessary for it to be kept informed as to *where all the Companies forming the Battalions of a County Regiment are centred* on Form No. XIV. (see Appendix 2).

New detachments, when formed, must either join some existing Company, or, if of sufficient strength, form a new Company.

22. In Counties where there is a County Regiment the only unit to be recognised as entitled to affiliation is the Company. If the Regimental Commandant is satisfied that a district starting a detachment has a potential recruiting strength for a Company, he can recognise the formation as a Company, and give them a reasonable time to raise the requisite number. If, on the other hand, the Regimental Commandant is not satisfied that a Company can be raised in the district in question, the detachment may be permitted to have its own drill centre and facilities for training, but must link up with another detachment to form a Company, and be under the same Committee and management and Company Officer as the Corps to which it is linked up. The Affiliation Form to be used should be the card (Form XIV.) County Edition, Revised (see Appendix 2), which serves all purposes. All cards must be forwarded to the Central Association. A duplicate should be kept at the Headquarters. *Definition of a Unit.* *C.A.V.T.C., 16/8/15, XLI.*

23. 1. Under the new Regulation of July, 1915, the Regimental Commandant is responsible for the Inspection and Affiliation of the Units under his Command by himself or an Officer detailed by him. *Instructions for the Inspection of County Regiments.* *C.A.V.T.C., 10/8/15.*

2. The Regimental Commandant or an Officer deputed by him must examine the Corps Register and other books of the Units, and see that all men of military age on the Register have signed the undertaking required by the War Office Letter dated the 19th November, 1914, reference 20/Gen. No./3604 (A.G.I.), and that all the Rules and Regulations of the Central Association are adhered to.

3. The Officer inspecting must fill up the Central Association's Inspection Form (No. XIII., revised August 9th, 1915, Appendix 5), and report as to the general training and discipline of the Corps inspected, such report being transmitted to, and filed at, the County Regimental Headquarters.

4. Special attention must be paid to the competency of the Officers in the Corps inspected, and the recommendation of the Regimental Commandant for their formal appointment by the Lieutenant of the County as President of the County Committee will depend on a satisfactory report as to their efficiency.

5. If the Regimental Commandant is satisfied with the report he will confirm the affiliation of the Unit, and when all the Units comprising a Battalion are reported on as satisfactory, the Battalion itself becomes affiliated. If the report reveals that the Unit inspected is unsatisfactory, the Regimental Commandant should recommend the County Committee to disaffiliate the Unit.

6. The C.A.V.T.C. will send an Inspecting Officer periodically to inspect the County Regiments, previous notice being given to the Regimental Commandant. This Inspecting Officer will visit the Headquarters of the Regiment and inspect the reports and records of the Regiment, and any unit he considers necessary. In case of unsatisfactory reports the Central Association reserves the right to cancel the affiliation of the whole, or part, of the Regiment.

Programme for Inspection **24**. Officers of Corps applying for inspection should submit a provisional programme of the proposed inspection to the Regimental Commandant, stating the probable strength on parade. This programme will be usually followed, but is liable to variation by the Regimental Commandant. It should be stated how far the place of inspection is from the railway station, and if a conveyance will be provided for the Inspecting Officer, also the probable time it will take to get there.

Inspection Report. **25**. Corps are not to receive a copy of the Inspection report, but the purport of it should be transmitted to the Corps officially. Attention is to be directed to any failure to comply with the Regulations, particularly in cases of men of military age who have not accepted the terms of the War Office letter of the 19th November, 1914.

26. There is no objection to the purport of the Inspecting Officer's report as transmitted to the Corps being communicated to the Press.

Press and Inspecting Officer's Reports.
C.A.V.T.C., 16/7/15.

27. Considerable inconvenience has been caused in the delay in returning the Cards supplied to County Adjutants for the Registration of Companies to the Central Association (Form XIV. County Edition, Revised, Appendix 2). The War Office expects to be kept supplied regularly with information as to the location of Units, with their Headquarters and correct numbers. These Cards must be filled up directly Companies are formed, so that the Central Association Register for every County may be kept up to date.

Registration Forms.
C.A.V.T.C., 16/8/15, XLI.

SUGGESTED SCHEME FOR A COUNTY VOLUNTEER REGIMENT.

28. 1. That a Volunteer Regiment be formed for the County of...................... under the auspices of the Lord Lieutenant and affiliated to the Central Association of Volunteer Training Corps, whose Rules shall be adhered to.

C.A.V.T.C 23/3/15, XXIV.

2. That a provisional Grand Council be formed and that the Lord Lieutenant be invited to act as President, and that each existing Corps should be entitled provisionally to one representative on such Council, that the High Sheriff of the County, Chairman of the County Council, the Chief Constable, the Chairman of the Territorial Association, the Mayors of all Municipal Boroughs and the Members of the Executive Committee, hereinafter mentioned, shall be *ex officio* members of the said Grand Council.

3. That the President of the Grand Council shall appoint a Regimental Commandant to organise, co-ordinate, control and be responsible for, the Volunteer Training Corps Movement throughout the County.

4. That the President of the Grand Council shall appoint a Regimental Adjutant to fulfil the duties of Adjutant to the County Regiment and discharge the duties of Honorary Secretary and to whom all correspondence concerning the County Volunteer Movement must be addressed.

5. That the Headquarters of the Regiment shall be at ....
....
....

6. That there shall be an Executive Committee responsible for the Finances, Military Organisation and Administration of the affairs of the County Regiment of which the Lord Lieutenant, Regimental Commandant, Regimental Adjutant, Battalion Commandants and Chief Constable of the County shall be *ex officio* members and to which three members shall be elected by the Grand Council.

7. That the basis of the Battalion Organisation shall be the Parliamentary Constituencies of the county*, and that the President of the Grand Council, in consultation with the Regimental Commandant, shall approve the appointment of Battalion Commandants to organise the Volunteer Corps into Battalions and to be responsible for the proper conduct and the good discipline of Corps under their control.

8. In connection with local detachments the duties of local Committees will be [with the sanction of the Battalion Commandant and the approval of the County Regimental Commandant] to raise, clothe and equip, if possible, these detachments in connection with which such Committees are formed. They will also be

---

* Or some other convenient districts.

responsible for the financial arrangements of the detachment. They will in no way be responsible for the training or discipline, which will be dealt with by the Commanding Officer of the detachment, in communication,
through the prescribed channel, with the Battalion
Commandant.

9. The object of the Volunteer Corps is primarily for
the defence and safety of the district and county in which
they are situated, but a Register must be kept of those
whose occupation will permit them in case of invasion
to serve in other parts of the United Kingdom or who are
prepared from time to time to undertake special duties
away from home. A Record should be kept of Members
who are prepared to do Guard Work at night and the
hours and number of evenings they can give to these
duties.

10. Each Corps must keep the proper Corps Register,
the form of which must be that provided by the Central
Association of Volunteer Training Corps or one approved
by the Battalion Commandant.

11. Only men can be accepted as members of Corps
who are over military age, or who if of military age can
show a genuine reason for not joining the Army. The
latter must show that they are not enrolling in a Volunteer Corps in order to avoid joining the Army, by signing an undertaking to enlist if specially called upon to
do so, as laid down in the War Office Letter to Lord Desborough, dated 19th November, No. 20/Gen.No./3640
(A.G.I.).

12. The Officer Commanding each company must fill
up the affiliation form required by the Central Association forthwith (Form XIV. County Edition, revised,
Appendix 2), and send it to the County Regimental
Headquarters to be forwarded to the Central Association
of Volunteer Training Corps.

13. Quarterly reports must be sent in duplicate to the
County Regimental Adjutant by the Battalion Com-

mandant, one copy of which must be sent to the Headquarters of the Central Association of Volunteer Training Corps. The form to be used is Form XI., Third Edition, September, 1915 (see Appendix), issued by the Central Association of Volunteer Training Corps.

14. The War Office Brassard will be issued to all corps on the recommendation of the Regimental Commandant. No arms can be carried nor can uniform be worn except this Brassard be worn on the left arm above the elbow. The name and company number of each man must be written clearly inside the Brassard, which must not be transferred: when he ceases to be a member of the corps the Brassard must be returned to the County Headquarters and destroyed.

15. Uniform must be within the regulations of the Central Association of Volunteer Training Corps, and the County pattern will be recommended by the Executive Committee to the Grand Council for approval. Uniform is not compulsory for a corps, but, if adopted, the County pattern must be worn. It can only be adopted if the Local Committee is in a position to complete the clothing of the Company Formation. Uniform can only be used on duty or going to and from parade.

16. Company and Platoon Commanders can be elected by the Committee or members of a corps always subject to the approval of the Regimental Commandant and to formal appointment by the County President.

17. The titles of Officers shall be as laid down by the Central Association of Volunteer Training Corps, see Form XXII.

18. Special Constables can only be accepted as members of a corps provided they understand that being attested as Special Constables their duty as Special Constables takes precedence over their duty as Volunteers. In case of invasion it will be for the Chief Constable to decide whether he can release them from their service as Special Constables.

19. The Volunteers cannot be attested, but men enrolling in a Volunteer Corps must undertake to loyally carry out the orders of their Superior Officers in the spirit of military discipline. Any case of insubordination will subject the Volunteer to instant dismissal from the County Regiment by the Battalion Commandant and the forfeiture of all right of membership. In such cases all equipment must be immediately handed over to the responsible Officer of the corps.

20. A proper register of drill attendances must be kept by each corps. Forty drills of not less than one hour each entitles a Volunteer to the Central Association of Volunteer Training Corps' Proficiency Badge, provided he is at least a second class shot according to classification.

Leaflet A 1. issued by the Central Association of Volunteer Training Corps lays down that:—

" It is not absolutely necessary for ex-Regulars and ex-Territorials to complete the full number of drills laid down as above before becoming entitled to these proficiency badges, provided the Commandant of their corps is satisfied with their general military knowledge in drill and shooting."

21. Should serviceable rifles be in possession of a corps, a proper armoury must be provided, and the necessary steps taken for the safe custody of the rifles and ammunition. Rifles must be returned to the armoury after parade.

22. A County Fund to be opened to which both individuals and corps in the county be invited to subscribe, the money so obtained to be used in the first place for defraying the necessary expenses, secretarial or otherwise, incurred by the Grand Council, and secondly to supplement the funds of the corps in poor districts and assist them in the purchase of arms and equipment.

C

COUNTY VOLUNTEER REGIMENTS.

The following is a list of County Volunteer Regiments formed to date.

County.	President.	Regimental Commandant.	Address for Official Communications.
BERKSHIRE ...	James Herbert Benyon	Brigadier-General W. A. Collings	Captain G. J. Metcalfe, The Knowle, Maidenhead.
BUCKINGHAMSHIRE	The Marquess of Lincolnshire, K.G., P.C., G.C.M.G.	The Marques of Lincolnshire, K.G., P.C., G.C.M.G.	C. E. A. Redhead, 7, Temple Square, Aylesbury.
CAMBRIDGESHIRE ...	... ...	... ...	Lieutenant-Colonel Louis Tebbutt, 4, Salisbury Villas, Cambridge.
CARMARTHENSHIRE	J. W. Gwynne-Hughes	Lieutenant-Colonel F. D. W. Drummond	Lieutenant-Col. F. D. W. Drummond, Cawdor Estate Office, Carmarthen.
CARNARVONSHIRE ...	John Ernest Greaves ...	Colonel C. E. Dixon ...	Isaac Edwards, 12, Market Street, Carnarvon.
CHESHIRE	The Duke of Westminster, G.C.V.O.	Colonel George Dixon, D.L.	Colonel Alan J. Sykes, M.P., 12, St. Peter's Square, Stockport.
CORNWALL	The Earl of Mount Edgcumbe, P.C., G.C.V.O.	Brigadier - General T. C. Porter, C.B.	Philip E. B. Porter, Saltash, Cornwall.
CUMBERLAND ...	Lord Muncaster	Colonel J. S. Ainsworth, M.P.	Captain Graham, London Joint Stock Bank, Whitehaven.
DENBIGHSHIRE ...	Colonel William Cornwallis-West	Honorary Commandant Colonel Wm. Cornwallis-West	D. MacNicoll, Derwas, Abergele.
DERBYSHIRE ...	The Duke of Devonshire, G.C.V.O.	The Duke of Devonshire, P.C., G.C.V.O.	Colonel H. Brooke Taylor, Town Hall Chambers, Bakewell, Derbyshire.

DEVONSHIRE ...	Sir E. Chaning Wills, BART.	General Sir Richard Harrison, K.C.B.	G. Hardy Harris, 25, Southernhay, Exeter.
DORSET ...	Colonel J. Mount Batten, C.B.	Colonel J. L. Tweedie, D.S.O.	Colonel J. L. Tweedie, County House, Dorchester.
ESSEX ...	Colonel the Earl of Warwick	Lieutenant-General Sir A. R. Martin, K.C.B.	Lieutenant-Colonel John Colvin, 57, Duke Street, Chelmsford.
FLINTSHIRE ...	Henry Nevill Gladstone	Colonel H. R. Lloyd Howard, C.B.	F. Llewellyn-Jones, B.A., LL.B., Solicitor, Mold, N. Wales.
GLAMORGAN ...	The Earl of Plymouth, C.B., P.C.	Major T. L. W. Lucas ...	H. Middleton, 75, St. Mary Street, Cardiff.
GLOUCESTERSHIRE ...	The Earl Beauchamp, P.C., K.G.	Colonel Cecil Davis ...	Theodore Hannam-Clark, 12, Queen Street, Gloucester.
HEREFORDSHIRE ...	Sir John Cotterell, BART.	Captain A. W. Foster ...	George Holloway, 17½, Victoria Street, Hereford.
HERTFORDSHIRE ...	The Viscount Hampden, P.C.	The Earl of Essex...	Wilfrid E. Laurie, Constabulary Headquarters, Hatfield.
HUNTINGDONSHIRE ...	The Earl of Sandwich, P.C., K.C.V.O.	Lord Charles Montagu ...	John Bell, Estate Office, Kimbolton Castle, Hunts.
ISLE OF WIGHT ...	The Lord Tennyson, P.C., G.C.M.G., D.L.	Sir Charles Seely, Bart. ...	W. Ormsby Rymer, Deputy Sheriff's Office, 33a, Holyrood Street, Newport, I.W.
KENT ...	Colonel the Lord Harris, G.C.S.I., G.C.I.E.	The Lord Harris, G.C.S.I., G.C.I.E.	H. Nicholson, Bidborough Hall, Tunbridge Wells.
LANCASHIRE ...	The Lord Shuttleworth	Sir James de Hoghton, BART.	The Commandant, Lancashire Volunteer Brigade, County Offices, Preston.
*LEICESTERSHIRE ...	The Lord Ranksborough	Colonel J. G. Bruxner-Randall	S. C. Packer, 2, Newarke Street, Leicester.
MIDDLESEX ...	Major-General the Lord Cheylesmore, K.C.V.O.	Colonel Bowles, Forty Hall, Enfield	H. Goadby, 91, Brook Green, W.
MONMOUTHSHIRE ...	Major-Gen. Sir I. J. C. Herbert, BT., M.P., C.B.	Lieutenant-Colonel E. B. Herbert	Lieut.-Col. A. H. Laybourne, c/o Isca Foundry, Newport.

* This county and the county of Rutland form one Regiment.

COUNTY VOLUNTEER REGIMENTS—*continued.*

County.	President.	Regimental Commandant.	Address for Official Communications.
NORFOLK	The Earl of Leicester, G.C.V.O., C.M.G.	The Earl of Leicester, G.C.V.O., C.M.G.	Malcolm Caley, Howard House, King Street, Norwich.
NORTHAMPTONSHIRE	The Earl Spencer, P.C., G.C.V.O.		W. H. Holloway, 14, Guildhall Road, Northampton.
NOTTINGHAMSHIRE	The Duke of Portland, K.G.	Colonel Sir Lancelot Rolleston, K.C.B., D.S.O.	H. Gover Ford, 1, King's Walk Chambers, Parliament Street, Nottingham
OXFORDSHIRE ...	The Duke of Marlborough	A. D. Godley	W. F. Cooper, Magdalen College, Oxford.
*RUTLAND	The Lord Ranksborough	Colonel C. Norcott, C.M.G.	Colonel C. Norcott, Wing House, Wing, Oakham.
SHROPSHIRE ...	The Earl of Powis ...	Captain Beville Stanier, M.P.	C. Inge Gardiner, 15, High Street, Shrewsbury.
SOMERSET ...	Lieut.-Colonel the Earl Waldegrave, V.D.	Colonel A. Thrale Perkins, C.B.	H. Byard, Sheppard, 8, Hammet Street, Taunton.
STAFFORDSHIRE ...	The Earl of Dartmouth, P.C.	Lord Stafford	Major J. Wilkins, Bilbrook Grange, Codsall, Staffs.
SUFFOLK	Colonel Sir Courtenay Warner, BT., C.B., M.P.	Earl Cadogan	Captain Russell K. Britain, County Hall, Ipswich.
SURREY	The Hon. Henry Cubitt, C.B.	General Sir Josceline Wodehouse, G.C.B., C.M.G.	Colonel G. A. Williams, Caxton House, Westminster, S.W.
SUSSEX	The Duke of Norfolk ...	The Duke of Norfolk, K.G., P.C.	Colonel E. A. Young, Wykeham Close, Steyning.
WARWICKSHIRE	The Earl of Craven ...	Colonel D. F. Lewis, C.B.	Battns. Nos. 1, 3, 4, 5; W. A. Grist, Cornwall Buildings, 49, Newhall, Birmingham; Batt. No. 2: Major Frank Glover, Church Walk, Royal Leamington Spa.

* This county and the county of Leicestershire form one Regiment.

County	President	Regimental Commandant	Address for Official Communications
WORCESTERSHIRE ...	The Earl of Coventry, P.C.	Lieutenant-Colonel A. H. Hudson	Lieut.-Col. J. Livingstone Wood, V.D., **Bank Buildings**, **Cross**, **Worcestershire.**
YORKSHIRE, E.R. ...	The Lord Nunburnholme, D.S.O.	Colonel W. Lambert White, V.D., D.L.	Col. George Easton, Staff Head-quarters, Paragon Buildings, Hull.
YORKSHIRE, N.R. ...	Sir Hugh ...ell, BART. ...	Colonel Sir J. D. Legard, K.C.B.	S. Ridge, Chancery **Lane**, Malton, Yorks.
YORKSHIRE, W.R. ..	The Earl of Harewood, K.C.V.O.	Brigadier-General A. Bewicke-Copley, C.B.	Lord Hawke, 14, Park Square, Leeds.

LONDON REGIMENTS.

County Commandant:—Gen. **Sir O'Moore Creagh**, V.C., G.C.B., G.C.S.T.

Hon. Secretary:—Percy A. **Harris**, C.A.V.T.C., Royal Courts of Justice, W.C.

County	President	Regimental Commandant	Address for Official Communications
EAST ...	The Marquess of Crewe, K.G.	Colonel Holman ...	Colonel Holman, 6, King's Bench Walk, Temple, E.C.
NORTH	,,	Brigadier-General Abbott, C.B.	Major Cyril Wood, 105, South Hill Park, Hampstead, N.W.
SOUTH	,,	Major-General Sir D. O'Callaghan, K.C.V.O.	Captain E. C. Baker, C.A.V.T.C., Royal Courts of Justice, W.C.
WEST ...	,,	Colonel S. Sankey, V.D. ...	Colonel S. Sankey, V.D., Guildhall, E.C.
CENTRAL	,,	Brigadier-General The Hon. F. C. Bridgeman, C.B.	Major J. H. Gordon Casserly, Imperial College Union, Prince Consort Road, South Kensington, W.

30. RANKS.

COUNTY ORGANISATION OF TWO OR MORE REGIMENTS.

Army Rank.	Corresponding V.T.C. Rank.
Brigadier-General - -	County Commandant (ranking senior to all Regimental Commandants).

REGIMENT CONSISTING OF TWO OR MORE BATTALIONS.

Army Rank.	Corresponding V.T.C. Rank.
Brigadier-General - -	Regimental Commandant.

When a County or Regimental Commandant is appointed and requires a Staff:—An Adjutant, a Quartermaster, each with the rank of Commandant or Sub-Commandant at the discretion of the County or Regimental Commandant, a Chaplain, a Medical Officer, and other Staff Officers as decided by the County or Regimental Commandant with such rank as he may allot, may be provided for the Headquarters of the County or Regiment. A Sergeant-Major and a Quartermaster-Sergeant may also be provided for a Regiment. All titles are used when on duty only. (See Para. 36 and 115.)

BATTALION of full regulation strength, as for the Regular Army, and of Four Double Companies.

Army Rank.	Corresponding V.T.C. Rank.
Lieutenant-Colonel Commanding - - -	Commandant.
Major - - - -	Sub-Commandant.
Captain, Commanding Company and Captain 2nd in Command of Company - - -	Company Commander.
Lieutenant or 2nd Lieutenant, Commanding Platoon - - -	Platoon Commander.

Army Rank.	Corresponding V.T C. Rank.
Adjutant - -	- Adjutant, ranking as Company or Platoon Commander as decided by the Regimental Commandant.
Quartermaster -	- Quartermaster, ranking as described above.
Chaplain - -	- Ranking as described above.
Medical Officer - -	ditto.

The Central Association has approved of the ranks of Squadron and Half Squadron Commander for Officers of the National Motor Volunteers. These ranks will correspond with those of Company and Platoon Commander respectively, and have the same badges of rank.

Signalling, Transport, Supply and Cyclist Officers may be appointed and seconded from the Battalion for these services, on the recommendation of the Battalion Commandant with the approval of the Regimental Commandant.

The Sub-Commandant takes the place of Commandant in the temporary absence of the latter, and, if the absence is permanent, a fresh Commandant should be appointed.

One Sub-Commandant to a Battalion is sufficient, and his rank of Sub-Commandant is intended to emphasise his position as second in Command.

A Sergeant-Major and a Quartermaster-Sergeant should be appointed to a Battalion.

A Company Sergeant-Major and a Company Quartermaster-Sergeant should be appointed to each Company and four Platoon Sergeants.

To each Platoon four Non-Commissioned Officers corresponding to the rank of " Sergeant " should be appointed and called " Section Commanders," also four " Section Corporals."

Military Rank.

31. The Association has no authority to grant the right to use military rank, neither can it refuse to allow an Officer to use military rank if he possesses such under proper authority.

No Commissions for Officers.

32. Commissions cannot be given to Officers in V.T.C., but a Form of Appointment has been approved by the Central Association for use by Presidents of County Associations.

Applications to serve as Officers.

33. A Volunteer wishing to serve as an Officer in any unit should forward his application, with all particulars regarding himself and previous training, to the Officer Commanding the Battalion with which he wishes to serve.

Appointment of Officers.

34. The formal appointment of officers rests with the President of the County Committee, who acts on the advice of the Regimental Commandant, to whom names of officers must be submitted by the Battalion Commandant. (See also Para. 28 (16) and Appendix 4.)

Before an Officer is confirmed in his appointment, and officially recommended to the County President for formal appointment, he should be able to show reasonable efficiency in tactics and interior economy, and satisfy both his Battalion and Regimental Commandant of his capacity for the rank he aspires to. If the Commandant is not satisfied with an Officer's qualifications, the Officer must go through a recognised Officers' Instructional class, or pass the examination of the Central Association Home Study Course. See also para. 129 (Officers' Instructional Classes) and para. 129A (Home Studies Course).

Honorary Rank.

35. When the Battalions have been organised, an Officer may be nominated as Honorary Battalion Commandant.

36. Regimental Adjutants, Quartermasters, Sergeant-Majors, and Quartermaster-Sergeants cannot have the prefix "Staff," but should have the word "Regimental" prefixed to their titles, which are to be used when on duty only. Staff.

37. A retired Officer of the Regular Army, Militia, Volunteer or Territorial Forces, having the right to retain his rank and being an Officer of a Volunteer Training Corps, may be addressed by both titles while on parade—thus, Company Commander Colonel Jones. Designation of Officers.

38. A Mayor can be appointed as *ex officio* Honorary Commandant of a Battalion. Honorary Commandant

39. The Honorary Secretary may be appointed an Officer, if acting as Regimental Battalion or Company Honorary Secretary, providing the Regimental Commandant sanctions the appointment. Honorary Secretary.

DISCIPLINE.

40. All Members must accept the conditions of their service prescribed by the Army Council and the C.A.V.T.C. Conditions of Service.

The greatest stress is to be laid on the importance of discipline, as being the foundation on which the structure of all efficient armed forces rests, and as the meaning of discipline is sometimes misunderstood, it should be borne in mind that it means the performance of duties in strict accordance with, not only the letter, but the spirit, of an order to the very best of every man's ability in every circumstance in which he may be placed.

41. Corps not following the Central Association Rules and Regulations will be disaffiliated. Disaffiliation

Relations between Volunteer Training Corps and the Regular, Reserve, and Territorial Forces.

42. The Volunteer Training Corps not being subject to military law, Officers and N.C.O.'s of the Volunteer Force have no power of command over Officers and N.C.O.'s of the Regular, Reserve, and Territorial Forces.

Volunteer Training Corps Units co-operating with troops subject to military law cannot become subject to military law by so doing, but by co-operating with them they will be held to have tacitly agreed to conform to the orders and instructions issued by the military authorities.

Duties of Regimental Commandant.

43. The Regimental Commandant will be responsible to the Central Association for the training and discipline of his units, and it will be his duty to see that the Rules and Regulations of the Central Association are carried out. He will consult and endeavour to meet, so far as possible, the wishes and convenience of Local Committees and Battalion Commandants. His authority will be supreme in all matters of training and discipline as well as in carrying out orders as to organisation and interior economy issued by the C.A.V.T.C. or the County Organisation. Where there are two or more Regiments in a county the title of County Commandant instead of Regimental Commandant can be used by the Commandant of the County.

Duties of Battalion Commandants.

44. Battalion Commandants will be responsible:—

(a) That all Regimental Orders are strictly complied with.

(b) That complete registers of Corps are kept up to date, and that all necessary returns are submitted.

(c) That a record is kept of each member's attendance at drills, camp, musketry, and field training, or any other form of instruction.

(d) That the discipline and general efficiency of his Battalion is maintained to the satisfaction of the Regimental Commandant.

45. During the absence of an Officer the next in seniority will take his place and carry out his duties. For this purpose it is necessary for Commandants of County Regiments to keep a Seniority Roll. This does not affect the right of a Regimental Commandant, with the approval of the President of the County Committee, nominating any Officer, regardless of seniority, to fill his place, should he see fit to do so.

Seniority Roll.

C.A.V.T.C., 16/8/15, XLI.

46. Where a member of a Committee is also a Volunteer serving in the Regiment, as far as Regimental discipline goes, his position on the Committee must not be allowed to interfere with his duty as a Volunteer.

Member of Committee.

47. No man shall be accepted as a member of any Unit of the Volunteer Training Corps who, less than three months previously, has been a member of any other Unit, except with the consent of his original Commanding Officer. "Previous Military Training, If Any?" (Paragraph 4 of Corps Register, Form XII., Appendix 1), shall be taken to include previous military service in a Volunteer Training Corps. It will be necessary, therefore, for all recruits to answer this question accordingly.

Change and Transfer.

C.A.V.T.C. 26/7/15.

48. Commandants of Corps must take the necessary steps to see that all members of the Corps between 19 and 40 years of age, including men up to 45 who have served in the Regular Army, Special Reserve, and the Volunteer or Territorial Forces for not less than one year, and who were discharged with a military character of not less than fair, sign Paragraph 7 of Corps Register, Form XII. (see Appendix 1). Until this is carried out Corps are not finally affiliated or recognised as being able to carry arms. They are also liable to have their provisional affiliation cancelled.

Signing Undertaking.

49. It has been generally laid down that Special Constables can join V.T. Corps provided it is clearly understood that their oath as a Constable takes precedence of

Special Constables.

their duty as a member of a Corps. In case of an invasion it will rest with the Chief Constable to decide whether they can be more profitably employed as Constables or Soldiers.

Disreputable Conduct.
50. In the case of men dressed in V.T.C. uniform and not belonging to an affiliated Corps, and bringing by their conduct the uniform into disrepute, the best course to pursue is to notify their behaviour to the Provost-Marshal and the Police.

Resignations
51. Any member of a Corps desiring to resign his membership must send in his resignation in writing to his Headquarters.

Saluting.
52. All members of Volunteer Corps when in uniform or wearing the Brassard, will conform as far as possible to Army discipline and practice, and, in particular, will salute Officers of their own Corps, as also Officers of the Navy, Army or Territorial Forces, or Officers of other Volunteer Corps when in uniform and conform to the usages of the Services. In most cases Officers of Volunteer Training Corps are saluted by Regulars out of courtesy, but such is not obligatory.

DRILL.

Infantry Training.
53. All drill and training of the V.T.C. is to be carried out on the lines of " Infantry Training, 1914 " (published by Messrs. Wyman and Sons, Ltd., Fetter Lane, London, E.C., price 6d.).

Efficiency.
C.A.V.C.T., 20/4/15.
54. Every member, before being returned as efficient, must have attended a minimum of forty drills of one hour each, and must at least be a second-class shot with Service sights at a Miniature Rifle Range, firing practice to count as a drill. For further particulars see Proficiency Badge. (Para. 105.)

Obligation to attend Drills.
C.A.V.T.C., 26/7/15,
55. The completion of forty drills does not do away with the obligation for Volunteers to continue to attend drills. A member of a Volunteer Corps who does not

attend a minimum of four drills per month shall be liable to be struck off the Roll of the Corps unless absent on leave given by the Commanding Officer of his Unit.

56. The following count each as one drill:—

A Recruit, Platoon or Company Drill

A Signalling Lesson,

A First Aid or Ambulance Lesson,

A Route March,

A Field Day,

A Church Parade, and

A Firing Practice.

Definition of a Drill.

57. No drill, whatever its duration, counts for more than one mark towards the Proficiency Badge, and no drill of less than one hour can be recognised.

Counting Drills for Proficiency Badge.

58. The period within which the forty drills necessary before obtaining the Proficiency Badge are to be completed is left to the discretion of the Officer Commanding the Unit.

Period for 40 Drills.

59. Men will not be permitted to drill with a Corps unless they are members of a V.T.C. or Special Constables, or guides enrolled under the County Territorial Association (see para. 73). This does not apply to recruits drilling with V.T.C. under Lord Derby's Scheme (see para. 75A).

Non-members drilling with V.T.C.

MISCELLANEOUS.

60. Membership of V.T.C. must be limited to natural-born or naturalised subjects of His Majesty.

Aliens. Army Council Ruling, 8/7/15.
20
Gen. No. 3937
(A.G.I.).

61.

Sir,—With reference to your letter of the 10th July, 1915, I am commanded by the Army Council to inform you that, provided he is otherwise eligible, there is nothing in the Regulations to prevent a National Reservist, registered in Class III., from joining a Volunteer Training Corps.

National Reservists, Class III.
Army Council Letter to Scottish V.T. Association, 13/7/15.
9
Reserve
4747
(A.G.I.)

I am, Sir,

Your obedient servant,

(Signed) B. B. CUBITT.

Guard Duties. **62.** Before any Corps undertakes to provide any members for guard or patrol duties, a written request from the proper constituted authorities must be obtained.

Military Age. **63.** The military age is from 19 to 40 years, *i.e.*, until **War Office Letter. Colonel Gosset. 1/10/15.** the 41st birthday is attained. In the case of men who have served in the Regular Army, Militia, Special Reserve, and the Volunteer or Territorial Forces for not less than one year, and who were discharged with a Military character of not less than "fair," the age (provided they are medically fit) is extended to 45—*i.e.*, until the 46th birthday is attained.

Lowest Age. **64.** The lowest age at which members of Volunteer Training Corps can be enrolled is the 17th birthday.

Mounted Units. **65.** Mounted Volunteer Force is the approved title for Mounted Units, but a Cavalry Unit cannot be sanctioned.

Infantry Corps. **66.** Volunteer Training Corps, with the exception of Engineer Companies, are to drill as Infantry Corps, except in special cases to be determined by the C.A.V.T.C.

Engineer Corps. **66a.** Engineer Corps can be formed, the company being taken as the recognised unit, but they must be linked up with their respective County Regiments, and recognise the command of their Regimental Commandant.

Corps Register. **67.** A Company or Platoon Commander may sign the Corps Register for the Commandant, provided he is authorised by him to do so.

Subscriptions **68.** Arrangements regarding subscriptions to Corps are matters on which the Central Association cannot advise; they must be decided according to local circumstances.

Women's Voluntary Aid Detachment. **69.** A Voluntary Aid Detachment for women may attach itself to the Ambulance Section of a Corps, provided the approval of the Regimental Commandant is first obtained.

70. Corps are warned that no camps or similar assemblies are to be held without the sanction of the General Officer Commanding-in-Chief of the Command in which the camp is proposed to be held.

The greater part of the Eastern Command is a prohibited area.

The limits of the various commands are given in the Army List.

Camps.

Headquarters Eastern Command, Whitehall, 21/7/15.

71. Cadet Companies can be formed of youths between the ages of 14 and 17, but such Companies are not entitled to the privileges of affiliation and can only be associated with Volunteer Corps for drill and training purposes. Such Cadet Companies cannot be supplied with the War Office Brassard. If uniform is worn the Cadets must have on their shoulders, in clear letters—V.T.C. CADETS—. From the age of 17 such Members come under the Regulations of the Central Association, and are therefore then entitled to wear the Brassard. All Cadets must state on the Corps Register whether they have been Members of another Cadet Corps, Church Lads' Brigade or Boy Scout Company. Commanding Officers must not take Cadets from another Corps without production of the official discharge certificate of a recognised Cadet Unit on Army Form E. 512, or within six months of being a member of another Corps, without the production of the consent, in writing, of his late Commanding Officer.

The above order is retrospective.

Cadet Companies

C.A.V.T.C., 26/7/15

72. Members of Volunteer Corps who desire to offer their services for week-end work in Munition Factories should do so as Members of the Corps to which they belong, and the Commanding Officers are recommended to form special Sections, Platoons or Companies, of men willing and able to do such work; and their services should be offered to the appropriate Authority as a Unit under their own Officer.

Munition Workers.

C.A.V.T.C. 26/7/15.

73. Guides enrolled under the County Territorial Association cannot be taken on the strength of Volunteer Corps, but should the Chief Guide so desire

Guides.

C.A.V.T.C., 16/8/15, XLI.

they can be attached for Drill, etc., provided that the first call on their Services is that of the Chief Guide. Nothing in this, however, prevents Scouts of Volunteer Corps being trained as Guides under the Rules already issued. (See para. 127.)

Strength.

74. Strength to be followed as in Regulations contained in the Field Service Regulations for the Army.

Lights for Night Marches, C.A.V.T.C., LII. Nov., 1915. 843001/2725.

74a. The attention of all Corps situated in the Metro politan area is called to letter dated 16th November, 1915 :—

"New Scotland Yard, S.W.

" Sir,

" I am directed by the Commissioner of Police of the " Metropolis to draw your attention to the fact that the " Military Authorities have recently issued an Order " that troops on the march at night shall carry a lantern " showing a white light at the head of the column and " another a red light at the rear.

"The Order was issued as the result of one or two " accidents having occurred to troops on the march at " night, and the Commissioner will be much obliged if " you will kindly notify the various Volunteer Corps " Units controlled by your Association of this fact, as " the adoption of similar precautions is very desirable " in cases where bodies of men travel in the roadway, " especially under the present conditions of lighting.

I am,
Sir,
Your obedient Servant,
(Signed) SUFFIELD MYLIUS."
" The Secretary,
" Central Association Volunteer Training Corps."

Correspondence.

75. The C.A.V.T.C. calls for no returns or information which are not absolutely necessary to enable it to comply with the orders of the military authorities. Periodical returns must be submitted on the specified dates and special returns asked for promptly sent in.

Letters should deal with one subject only. Unnecessary correspondence should be avoided. All correspondence should be submitted through the proper channel, which is as follows:—

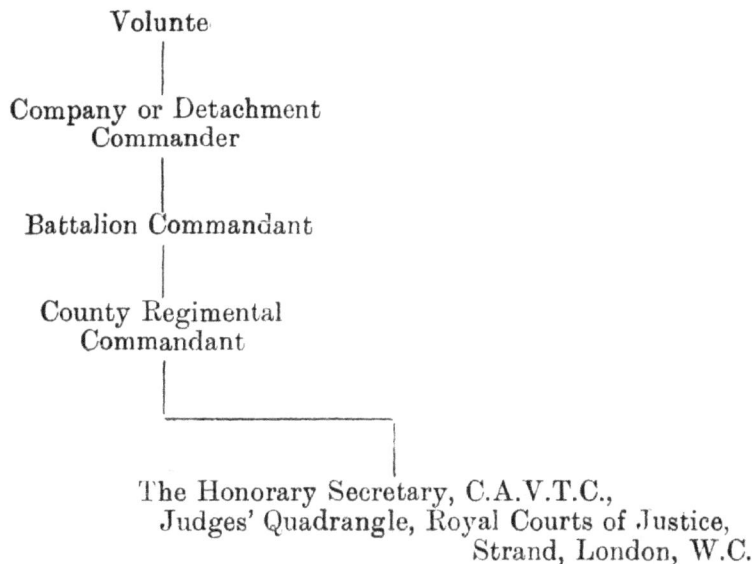

Volunteer
|
Company or Detachment
Commander
|
Battalion Commandant
|
County Regimental
Commandant
|

The Honorary Secretary, C.A.V.T.C.,
Judges' Quadrangle, Royal Courts of Justice,
Strand, London, W.C.

N.B.—Where no County Regiment exists communications for C.A.V.T.C. should be forwarded through Commandant of Corps.

75a. (1) All men enlisted in "Section B, Army Reserve," must be entered in a special Corps Register or Long Roll, whether members of Corps or attached for training only. This can be obtained in book form for 1s. 3d. each in books of 50, and 1s. 9d. each in books of 100, from the Central Association. *Recruits under Lord Derby's Scheme.*

(2) In the case of men who are already members of the Corps, an entry "Section B, Army Reserve," should be made in red ink across the ordinary Corps Register Form which he has already signed, and he must also be entered in the special Corps Register for "Section B, Army Reserve."

D

(3) Men enlisted in " Section B, Army Reserve," under Lord Derby's Scheme can be " attached " for training purposes only, in which case they must not be provided with the G.R. Red Brassard, and not counted on the Corps' strength. Members of Volunteer Corps enlisted in " Section B, Army Reserve," may wear the Volunteer uniform with the Red Brassard. When not on duty they should not wear the Red Brassard, but the Khaki Armlet.

SECTION III.

UNIFORM, EQUIPMENT, ETC.

SECTION III.

UNIFORM, EQUIPMENT, ETC.

BRASSARDS.

76.

"My Lord,—It having been represented that there is some doubt as to the object of the Brassard (Red Armlet with the letters G.R. inscribed therein) which was sanctioned for members of recognised Organisations of Volunteer Forces, etc., by War Office letter, number as above, of the 19th November, 1914, I am commanded by the Army Council to inform you that this Brassard is authorised as a general indication that the Corps has official sanction and as a mark of recognition of the individual to whom it is issued. To prevent misuse by transfer, the name of the individual should be indelibly inscribed on it.

"I am to add that the Council hold that the Brassard should always be worn when any military exercises or duties are being performed. Volunteer Associations who have not affiliated to the Central Association are not entitled to wear the Brassard.

"I am, My Lord,

"Your Lordship's obedient servant,

"(Signed) B. B. CUBITT.

"The Rt. Hon. Lord Desborough, K.C.V.O., President, Central Association Volunteer Training Corps, London, W.C."

Side note: Conditions of wearing Brassard. Letter from Army Council 20/4/15. General Number 3604 (A.G.I.)

Issue of Brassards. **77.** Where there is a County Organisation, Brassards are issued by the War Office on the order of the Central Association to Regimental Commandants, who transmit them to Units provisionally affiliated. Where there is no County Organisation, they may be issued to Corps provisionally affiliated on the recommendation of one of the following gentlemen : —

> Lord-Lieutenant of County,
> Lord Mayor or Mayor of Town,
> Officer Commanding the District,
> Chief Recruiting Officer,
> Chief Constable,
> Central Association Inspecting Officer.

Retired Officers wearing Brassards. **78.** Retired Officers of the Army, Territorials, or Volunteers, etc., entitled to wear the uniform of their old Regiment must not (if they are Officers of the V.T.C., and elect to wear their Army uniform) wear Brassards, as by the King's Regulations such addition to their authorised uniform is not permitted.

Brassard— Restrictions as to issue. **79.** Brassards must only be issued to those Members whose Enrolment Forms have been duly completed.

Brassards not to be altered.

C.A.V.T.C., 16/8/15. (X.L.I.) **80.** The Brassard must be worn as made, five inches wide, this being in accordance with the requirements of the Hague Convention. The Brassard must not on any account be altered in shape or form, and no badges of any kind must be worn on it.

Brassards to contain Name and Number. **81.** Each man's name and regimental number must be placed on Brassards (inside).

Destroying Brassards. **82.** When Brassards are returned to Headquarters on a man leaving the Corps, they must be destroyed, the Commandant being responsible that this is done.

Brassard always worn on Parade. **83.** Corps Officers and Members are desired to note that, notwithstanding anything that may have been said to the contrary, the official Brassard or Armlet must be worn when a Corps is on parade, whether in uniform or in private dress.

84

" Sir,—With reference to your letter PAH/LS of the 29th ultimo, I am commanded by the Army Council to inform you that the Brassards supplied to the Central Association Volunteer Training Corps, in accordance with paragraph 4 of War Office letter of the 19th November, 1914, for the use of members of Corps affiliated to the Central Association are the property of the State, and cannot therefore be allowed to pass into the private ownership of individual members.

Brassards the Property of the State.

20

Gen. No.
8604
(Q.M.G. 7.)
War Office,
London,
S.W.
18th August
1915.

" The Council trust that adequate steps are taken to ensure that the Brassards are recovered from those individuals who on leaving a Corps are no longer entitled to retain them. Used Brassards, being marked with the name of the member to whom they were issued, will, after return, be burnt in the presence of a responsible official, who should retain a record of those so destroyed.

" In the event of an ex-member declining to return the Brassard after reasonable application, the assistance of the civil authority can be invoked.

" It will be understood that any improper use of the Brassard renders the offender liable under the Defence of the Realm Act.

" I am, Sir,

" Your obedient Servant,

" (Signed)   B. B. Cubitt.

" The Honorary Secretary, Central Association
Volunteer Training Corps, Judges' Quadrangle,
Royal Courts of Justice, W.C."

UNIFORMS.

85. The Uniform approved by the Military Committee of the Central Association Volunteer Training Corps is a Norfolk Jacket, with shoulder straps, made in a green-grey rainproof drill. For Non-Commissioned Officers and men it must be made with a closed collar and Military cuff; for Officers with open neck to show tie, and

Form XVI.
Revised.

C.A.V.T.C.
8/2/13.

plain sleeves so that bands can be worn. The rank of
the Officer should be indicated by Braid Bands worn
on the cuff. This coat, where possible, should be
worn with Breeches or Trousers made of Whipcord or the
same material as the Coat, brown leather Gaiters and
Boots. Putties may be worn instead of Gaiters. A
leather belt can be worn instead of belt of the same
material as the Jacket; and the Cap, where obtainable,
should be the ordinary Military Peak Cap, but no objection would be made to the Forage Cap or Felt Hat; but
the headgear should be decided upon by each Corps. The
Military Committee recommend that the Norfolk Jacket
should be made full so that it can be worn over thick
Clothes or a Cardigan Jacket. It is also suggested that,
if it can be afforded, the Jacket should be lined. Where
there is a County Regiment a County Uniform should be
designed, conforming to the rules of the Central Association. Where there is a County pattern, it should be
made obligatory, except where modification is permitted
by the County Committee.

Woollen Cloth.
Form XIX.
War Office
Order.
2/2/15.
B.M. 19/55.
(Q.M.G.7)

86. Corps are prohibited from placing orders for
Uniforms to be manufactured from woollen Cloth.
" Cotton drill and cords will be found satisfactory and
sufficient."

Cotton and Woollen Bye-products
The War Office,
11/8/1915.
Reference
20
⎯⎯⎯⎯⎯
General
Number
3989
(Q.M.G.7.)

87. There is no objection to the use of the Cloth composed solely of a mixture of cotton and woollen bye-
products, as sanctioned for use by the Kent Volunteer
Fencibles, and the Regulations as regards Uniform contained in Form XIX. (para. 86) are extended accordingly.

Cadets.
C.A.V.T.C,
8/7/15.

88. Cadet Corps associated with the Central Association wishing to wear a uniform can do so, but the words
" V.T.C. Cadets " must be worn on the shoulder.

Cadet
Uniforms.
War Office
Letter,
29/3/15.
————————
9
————— Cadets
1761
(Q.M.G. 7.)

89. Officers of Cadet Corps attached to the Regular Army who may also be members of the V.T.C. must not wear their Military Uniform when appearing in public in connection with V.T.C. Corps.

90. Shoulder titles for shoulder straps in Volunteer Corps must include the letter " V."

Shoulder
Straps.

91. Retired Officers may wear the Uniform of their old Regiment if they are entitled and elect to do so; but it is desirable they should wear the Uniform of the Corps they are serving with as Officers, so as to be as little different from the men as possible.

Uniform for
Retired
Officers.

92. Where Uniforms differing from the authorised pattern were in existence prior to the issue of the form XVI., para. 85, relating to Uniform, Units may be allowed to retain them subject to special permission being given by the Central Association who may require modifications. In every such case the Uniform must satisfy War Office Regulations of 19th November, 1914, and be easily distinguishable from that worn by the Regular Army.

Uniforms
differing
from
Authorised
Pattern.

93. No Uniform must be worn except when necessary for training, but Volunteers attending a drill or parade may, if it is impossible to change into civil clothing, proceed to and from their place of business in Uniform.

Uniform
worn only for
Training.

94. Uniform must not be worn privately nor at places of public entertainment and restaurants.

Uniform
must not
be Worn
Privately.

95. Attendance at Church Parade and Recruiting Meetings when engaged on recruiting duty would justify the wearing of Uniform.

Church
Parade and
Recruiting
Meetings.

96. If the Chaplain is a private he should wear a private's Uniform, but if an Officer he should wear the prescribed Uniform substituting a clerical collar and black stock for the green shirt collar and tie, and he should wear the badges of his rank as an Officer.

Chaplain's
Uniform.

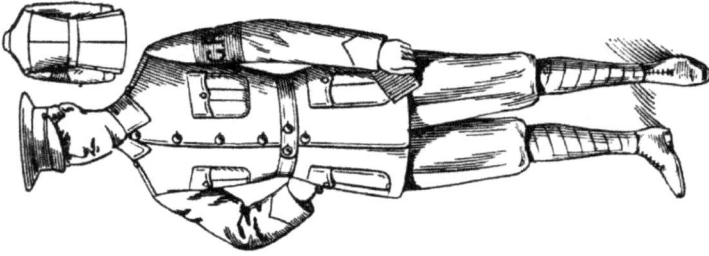

PRIVATE.
(Permissible Alternative Style.)

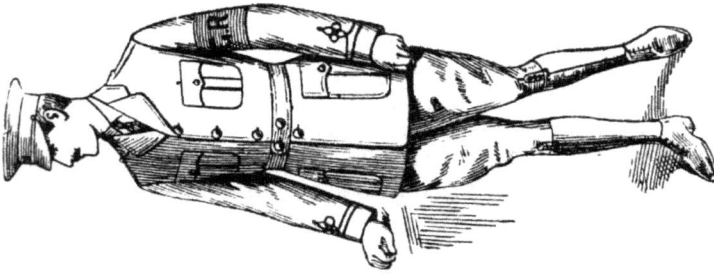

OFFICER.
(The Rank Mark is that of a
Company Commander.)

UNIFORMS.

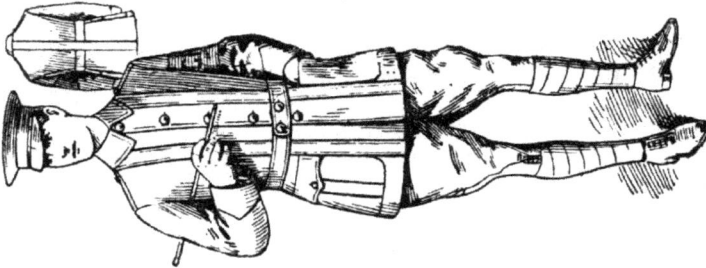

PRIVATE.
Original Pattern.)

Shoulder
Strap

PRIVATE.   OFFICER.

GREAT COATS.

Inspecting
Officer's
Uniform.

97. There is no obligation on the part of Inspecting Officers to wear Uniform, but if such is done they should wear that to which they are entitled. Corps prefer the Inspecting Officer to be in Uniform.

Honorary
Command-
ant's
Uniform.
C.A.V.T.C.
29/7/15.

98. An Honorary Commandant of a Battalion may wear the Uniform and take the rank of a Battalion Commandant, and when in Uniform should wear the Brassard.

BADGES OF RANK.

C.A.V.T.C.
XXII.

99. Badges of Rank should be worn on both sleeves below the elbow.

County Commandant	2 Rings; 1 Plain and the upper one an Austrian Knot. For difference in width of braid, see end of paragraph.
Regimental Commandant	5 Rings; 4 Plain and the upper one an Austrian Knot.
Commandant	4 Rings; 3 Plain and the upper one an Austrian Knot.
Sub-Commandant	3 Rings; 2 Plain and the upper one an Austrian Knot.
Company Commander and Squadron Commander (National Motor Volunteers).	2 Rings; 1 Plain and the upper one an Austrian Knot.
Platoon Commander and Half Squadron Commander	1 Ring, with Austrian Knot.
Adjutant	According to Rank.
Quartermaster	ditto.
Chaplain	ditto.
Medical Officer	ditto.

NON-COMMISSIONED OFFICERS.

Regimental Sergeant-Major	4 Plain Rings with One Disc an inch above the upper Ring.

Regimental Quarter-master Sergeant	3 Plain Rings with One Disc an inch above the upper Ring.
Battalion Sergeant-Major	4 Plain Rings.
Battalion Quartermaster-Sergeant	3 Plain Rings.
Company Sergeant-Major	2 Plain Rings with Three Discs an inch above and parallel to upper Ring and half-an-inch apart.
Company Quartermaster Sergeant	2 Plain Rings with Two Discs as above.
Platoon Sergeant - -	2 Plain Rings and One Disc.
Section Commander, ranking as Sergeant	2 Plain Rings.
Section Corporal - -	1 Plain Ring.

NOTE.—The Braid used for the rings must be for the County Commandant $1\frac{1}{2}$ inches in width for the lower ring only, the Austrian knot to be of the same size as for other ranks; in the case of other ranks the braid for the rings and Austrian knot must not be more than half an inch in width, and of any suitable colour. The discs to be of the same braid, and to be each fifteen-sixteenths of an inch in diameter (the size of a shilling).

BADGES.

100. Commandants of Regiments are requested to see that all Central Association Badges are issued through their Regimental Headquarters. Such badges should be obtained from the C.A.V.T.C. Offices.

Badges must be Official. C.A.V.T.C., 27/8/15.

101. No Badge must be worn which would tend to do away with the distinction between a Regular Uniform and a Volunteer Uniform, consequently any Badges bearing a similarity to those authorised for Regiments of the Regular Army are forbidden. In any case, permission for the use of Town, City or County Arms, or similar insignia, must be obtained from the authority to which they belong.

All Badges Distinct from Regular Army.

The Crown   **102**. The Crown as part of a Padge cannot be adopted without the sanction of the King.

The Bugle.   **103**. The Bugle, being a Light Infantry Badge, must not be worn by Volunteers.

Badges not worn by Officers.   **104**. It is not the custom in the Army for Officers to wear Badges other than Badges of rank, and this precedent must be followed in the Volunteers.

The Proficiency Badge   **105**. The sketch reproduced here illustrates the Proficiency Badge prepared for the Central Association by Mr. Solomon J. Solomon, R.A.

The above has received the approval of H.M. the King, who has graciously accepted a reproduction in gold. It is drawn to scale, and is exactly twice the size of the original. The Badge is oval with gilt frame, having the words Central Association V.T.C. embossed, surmounted by a royal crown. In the centre is a gilt embossed head of Bellona, the Goddess of War, with a background of black enamel. It can be supplied by the Central Association, at 1s. each or 11s. per dozen, for the use of members of Corps who are qualified to wear it.

Every member before being returned as efficient must have attended a minimum of forty Drills of one hour each, and must at least be a second-class Shot with Service sights at a Miniature Rifle Range, firing practice to count as a drill. Classification to be as follows:—

DELIBERATE.

Marksmen ... ... 95 per cent.
1st Class ... ... 90 ,,
2nd Class ... ... 85 ,,

Number of rounds to be fired is 10 with open sights only, C.A.V.T.C. Target, 2 in. bull: Distance 25 yards at a miniature range.

RAPID.

Marksmen ... ... 90 per cent.
1st Class ... ... 85 ,,
2nd Class ... ... 80 ,,

Time allowed: 100 Seconds for 10 rounds.

Similar Target to be used for both Deliberate and Rapid, and all Targets must be signed by the Range Officer before firing.

All Scores to be entered by Range Officer in his Book for further reference.

A special Target is now approved by the C.A.V.T.C. for 20-yard ranges with 1½ in. bull, to be obtained from Society of Miniature Rifle Clubs, Arundel House, Arundel Street, W.C,

Proficiency
Badge, only
badge to be
worn with
plain clothes.
Letter from
Army Council
23/10/15.
20
Gen. No.
405u
(Q.M.G.7.)

C.A.V.T.C.,
1/11/15.
XLIX.

105a.

War Office,

London, S.W.

23rd October, 1915.

" Sir,

" With reference to your letter PAH/LS of the 20th
" ultimo, I am commanded by the Army Council to
" inform you that approval is given for the use of the
" modified design of proficiency badge therein referred
" to, *i.e.*, a badge of the original pattern but with a gilt
" cameo head on a black background in substitution for
" a white enamel head on a blue background.

" I am to observe that this proficiency badge is the
" only badge approved by the Council for wear with
" plain clothes by members of Volunteer Corps affiliated
" to the Central Association Volunteer Training Corps,
" and that no alteration of the design or colouring of
" this badge may be made without the Council's
" authority

" I am further to point out that under Regulation 41
" of the Defence of the Realm Act the prohibition of the
" wearing of unauthorised badges adopted locally by
" Corps must be strictly enforced.

I am,

Sir,

Your obedient Servant,

(Signed)   B. B. CUBITT.

" The Hon. Secretary, C.A.V.T.C."

Local Badges.   **105b.** The following letter has been received from the
War Office since the issue of the last edition of these
Regulations confirming the right of Volunteers to wear
the Proficiency Badge, but stating they cannot modify
the Munitions (War Service Badges) Rules, 1915, as
regards the wearing by V.T.C.'s of local badges in
mufti ;—

War Office, London, S.W.

21st November, 1915.

20
Gen. No.
4050
(Q.M.G.7.)
C.A.V.T.C.,
LII.
19/11/15.

" SIR,—

" With reference to your letter PAH/LS of the 15th
" instant regarding button-hole badges introduced
" locally by Volunteer Training Corps without authority,
" I am commanded by the Army Council to observe that
" a proficiency badge has been approved and authorised
" for all Corps affiliated to the Central Association, and
" the Council regret therefore they cannot accord
" recognition to any badges which have been locally
" adopted.

" Local badges in some instances infringe the
" Munitions (War Service Badges) Rules, 1915, and in
" others bear crowns and other insignia which may not
" rightly be adopted without authority. Having
" approved a badge which is common to all Corps, the
" Council cannot afford general recognition to all the
" badges that may have been indiscriminately intro-
" duced.

" Further, it has been found necessary to prohibit
" the wearing during the period of the war of all
" National Reserve and Cadet badges which were
" authorised a long time before the present situation
" arose. The ruling conveyed to you in the last para-
" graph of War Office letter of the 23rd ultimo must be
" upheld and this decision must be accepted as final.

I am, Sir,

Your obedient Servant,

(Signed)   B. B. CUBITT.

" The Hon. Secretary,
" Central Association Volunteer Training Corps."

106. In carrying out the musketry tests for efficiency *Musketry*
—Rapid Fire—it is to be noted that the prescribed time, *Tests.*
viz., 100 seconds, is to count from the time that the man,
in the ready position with rifle loaded, receives the order
" Commence."

E

Issue of Proficiency Badges. **107.** Where there is a County Regiment, Proficiency Badges will be issued in bulk to Regimental Commandants on submission of indents and payments of cost. The Central Association leaves the distribution of these badges in the hands of Regimental Commandants, who will follow the Regulations issued from time to time with reference to these honourable distinctions. The Badges are specially to be worn in mufti, but may be worn in uniform with the sanction of Regimental Commandants, and when so worn they will be on the right breast on the same level as medals. It is recommended that Regimental Commandants should specify the number of Badges required with brooch pins for attaching to uniforms. In any case only one Badge must be issued to one man. Substitutes of the authorised Badge for proficiency are prohibited.

Marksman's Badge. **108.** A Badge has been designed and approved for Marksmen, and it is to be worn on the right sleeve below the elbow when in uniform or when there is no uniform when wearing the Brassard.

First Class Shots. **109.** A Badge has been designed and approved for First Class Shots, and is to be worn on the right sleeve below the elbow when in uniform or when there is no uniform when wearing the Brassard.

DESIGN OF BADGE FOR MARKSMEN.
Approved and Issued by the Central Association V.T. Corps.
(Full Size.)

A. Green-Grey Normal Tint.

B. Green-Grey, Dark.

C. Red.

D. Green-Grey, Light Tint.

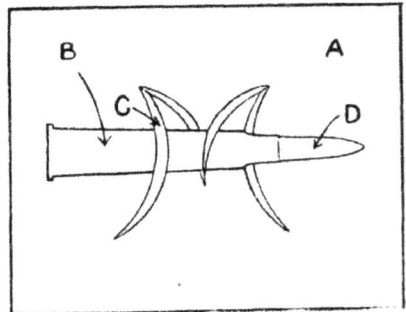

Badge for First-Class Shot is similar to above, but without the letter M.

110. A flag in blue and white has been designed and Signalling Badge. approved for members of Signalling Sections, and such is to be worn on the right sleeve above the elbow when in uniform or when there is no uniform when wearing the Brassard.

SIGNALLING BADGE.

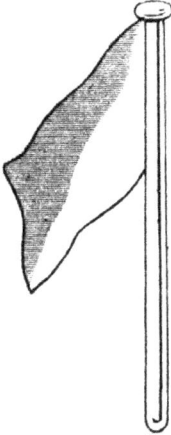

Designed and approved by the Central Association Volunteer Training Corps.

The flag is divided into blue and white halves. The staff and border are in light grey-green, and the whole design is mounted on a grey-green background.

The badge can be obtained only from the Central Association.

The above Badge is not to be issued or worn until an examination, which will be arranged by the Regimental Commandant, particulars of which are given below, has been passed to his satisfaction.

EXAMINATION FOR SIGNALLING BADGE.

111. The C.A. has approved of the amended standard Examination for Signalling. examination for Signallers, particulars of which are given below. This amended standard is in substitution for the former Para. 111, which is hereby cancelled.

SYLLABUS OF EXAMINATION IN SIGNALLING.

Morse Flag, Semaphore Flag, and Lamp (or alternatively Buzzer).

Size of Flags.

Morse and semaphore—2 ft. by 2 ft., with 3 ft. 6 in.
pole.

[NOTE.—Silk flags will not be permitted in examination tests.]

General Tests.

(1) A knowledge of the difference in procedure
between moving and fixed stations.

(2) Selection of positions for stations:—

(*a*) Facility for obtaining communication.
(*b*) Concealment from hostile forces.
(*c*) Use of blue and white flags.
(*d*) Background.
(*e*) Skylines, advantages and disadvantages of signalling upon.

(3) Allocation and duties of men at stations.

(4) Duties of Signal Officers.

(5) General principles of communication work.

(6) Procedure in connection with receipt and delivery
of messages and knowledge of message form, including
the counting of words, meaning of special symbols,
method of writing, the signalling and repetition of
figures, cypher groups, codes and prefixes.

Signalling Tests.

(1) MORSE FLAG—

(*a*) Send and read 78 letters (three alphabets in 20
groups) in 2 minutes 15 seconds.
(*b*) 40 words (200 letters) in 8 minutes.
(*c*) Read two test messages from the Examiner.

(2) SEMAPHORE FLAG—

(*a*) Send and read 78 letters (three alphabets in 20
groups) in 1 minute 45 seconds.

(*b*) Send and read 40 words (200 letters) in 4 minutes.

(*c*) Read two test messages from the Examiner.

Distance between reader and sender to be between 400 and 500 yards.

(3) LAMPS (or alternatively BUZZER)*—

(*a*) Send and read 78 letters (three alphabets in 20 groups) in 2½ minutes.

(*b*) 20 words (100 letters) in 4 minutes.

(*c*) Read two test messages from the Examiner.

Distance between reader and sender to be between 400 and 500 yards (this refers to lamp only).

Under the tests grouped under " General Tests," the qualifying standard must be at least 75 per cent. of the maximum marks.

Signallers will be classified upon the results of the above tests : —

First-class—Very accurate = 98 per cent.

Second-class—Accurate = 95 per cent.

Failed—Below 95 per cent. (See also para. 129B, Signalling Classes.)

---

* Buzzer signalling shall be allowed as an alternative to lamp.

A man who can send on the Buzzer could send equally well on the Lamp, while the Buzzer would probably be more useful in connection with communications by means of the combined telephone and buzzer sets used in cable work, and less likely to be banned.

Some Volunteer Corps have been practising on buzzers whilst others have adopted lamp signalling—the Morse c)de is used in connection with both, and it would be an advantage to have men trained in buzzer working, as they could, with a little practice, undertake telegraph sounder operating duties.

NOTE.—The above Syllabus of Examination may be amended from time to time, as occasion arises.

Cyclists' Badges.

111a. A Badge in khaki bronze has been approved for members of Cyclist Sections, and such is to be worn on the left sleeve of the uniform jacket, below the elbow. These Badges can only be obtained from the Central Association V.T. Corps, at 1s. each or 11s. per dozen. Design as above reproduced in actual size.

Bandmaster and Band.

112. The Badges of rank of a Bandmaster should be those according to his rank in the Corps. There is no special Badge of rank authorised. Bandsmen's shoulder wings are permitted for members of a band. They must be of the colour of the uniform, ornamented with braid the same colour as the facings, or where no facings exist of similar braid to that used for Badges of Rank.

The enrolment of Bandsmen as members of Volunteer Training Corps, and the wearing of uniform by such members, is a matter to be determined by Regimental Commandants, but Bandsmen are not to wear the Brassard unless enrolled as members of Corps.

Red Cross.

Army Council 18/6/15.

113. In reference to Ambulance Sections this Association has received, under Number 82/1224 (C.2.), dated 18th June, 1915, the following :—

" I am commanded by the Army Council to say that they regret that they are unable to grant permission to the Ambulance Bearer Sections attached to your Corps to use the Red Cross Badge."

Ambulance Sections must discontinue the use of Red Cross Badges, except as provided in Field Ambulance Regulations 130A (9).

114. The Ambulance Badge of the Association to be worn on the right sleeve above the elbow is as under. (See para. 130A, Field Ambulance Rules and Regulations.)

Ambulance Badge.
16/8/15,
XLI.

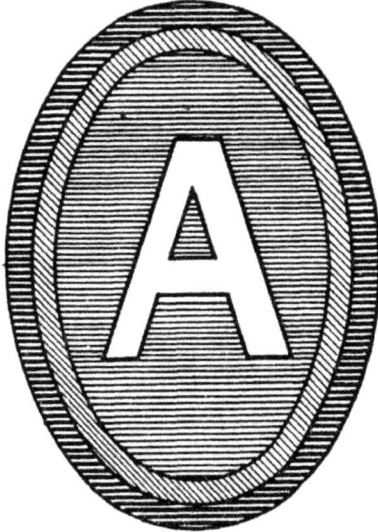

115. Regimental Officers doing Staff duty should wear a bronze letter " S " half an inch in height on each lapel of the V.T.C. uniform jacket. It is to be mounted on a patch $1\frac{1}{4}$ inches in diameter, of the same colour as the facings, where such exist; where there are none, the patch is to be formed of braid of the same material and colour as the Badges of Rank. Modifications in colour may be made with the sanction of the Regimental Commandant, but in no case is red or scarlet to be used. This does not, however, apply to the Staff of a Battalion. A gorget patch, being a Badge of the Regular Army Staff, cannot be worn.

Staff Badge.

116. Bronzed Badges of County Regiments and Battalions may be worn on the shoulder straps if of a design approved by the Regimental Commandant and the Central Association.

County Badge.

Town, City, or County Arms. **117.** Town, City or County Arms, or similar insignia, may be worn on the cap and collar, providing the consent of the authority concerned is obtained.

Badges may be worn on duty without Uniform. **118.** Should members have no uniform, Badges of Rank or other Badges authorised by the Association may be worn over private clothes when on duty only attached to small armlets of the regulation grey-green colour, which may be worn on the cuff. No Badge, except the Proficiency Badge, may be worn on any occasion without the Brassard. (See para. 105A B.)

MISCELLANEOUS.

Colours. **119.** It is not considered desirable for Volunteer Training Corps to carry Colours, as it is not now the tendency of Regular Regiments to take colours on service.

Camp Colours **120.** For camps a Flag of a grey-green colour may be adopted, bearing the abbreviated title of the Regiment or Battalion upon it with the addition of the letters "V.T.C.," and the distinguishing Battalion Numeral :—

V.T.C.
BUCKINGHAM COUNTY.

Would mean—
The Buckinghamshire County Regiment Headquarters.

V.T.C.
1
DERBY COUNTY

Would mean—
The 1st Battalion of the Derbyshire County Regiment Headquarters.

The insertion of "shire" after the name of the county is left to the discretion of the County Committee.

121. Sam Browne Belts may be worn by Officers as a part of the Uniform. Sam Browne Belts.

122. Swords may be worn by Officers on duty if the Unit to which they are attached possesses Rifles. Swords

123. The following letter has been received from the Home Office in reference to gun licences:— Gun Licences. Home Office Letter to C.A.V.T.C., 16/8/15.

" As I informed you some days ago, I sent your
" letter of the 4th August, on the subject of gun licences
" for members of the Volunteer Training Corps, to the
" Board of Inland Revenue. I am now informed that
" the Board no longer deals with questions of gun
" licences, but that the proper authority is the London
" County Council. I find, however, that the War Office
" has officially expressed the view that a Member of a
" Volunteer Training Corps affiliated to the Central
" Association of Volunteer Training Corps, and there-
" fore recognised by the Army Council, is ' a person in
" ' the Naval, Military or Volunteer service of His
" ' Majesty,' and therefore exempted under Section 7
" (1) of the Gun Licences Act, 1870. This probably
" meets the point raised in your letter."

124. The following communication has been received from the War Office on the subject of rifles:— Rifles. War Office, London, S.W. 26/8/15. 20 ——— Gen. No. 3604 (A.G.I.)

Sir,—I am commanded by the Army Council to inform you that those Volunteer Corps which are affiliated to the Central Association Volunteer Training Corps may provide themselves, at their own expense, with rifles, under local and individual arrangements, under the following conditions:—

(a) Rifles should be of a non-Service pattern, but capable of firing Service Ammunition. The maximum price must not exceed £2 10s. per rifle.

(b) The price paid for ammunition must not exceed £5 per 1,000 rounds.

(c) No responsibility can be accepted by the War Office in regard to the safety of rifles and ammunition so purchased. They may be of a quality which would not be accepted in the Service.

(d) If at any time the labour, machinery, or material used for the production of these rifles of a non-service pattern can be made available for Service purposes, or if it is found that the purchase of rifles and ammunition in any way interferes with the supplies of the Ministry of Munitions, it may be necessary to take steps which would have the effect of preventing the supplies of either article reaching the Volunteer Training Corps.

I am, Sir,

Your obedient Servant,

(Signed)   B. B. Cubitt.

The Hon. Secretary,
Central Association
Volunteer Training Corps,
Judges' Quadrangle,
Royal Courts of Justice, W.C.

C.A.V.T.C.
28/9/15.

Under orders from Headquarters, Southern Command, Salisbury, dated 14th September and 27th September, 1915, Volunteer Corps buying rifles or ammunition from any factories or dealers in the area of the Southern Command must make application to the Adjutant-General, Southern Command, such application to be first endorsed by the Central Association Volunteer Training Corps.

SECTION IV.

TRAINING AND EDUCATION.

SECTION IV.

TRAINING AND EDUCATION.

DUTIES OF VOLUNTEER TRAINING CORPS.

125. Though the duties of Volunteer Training Corps cannot be definitely laid down, their first and foremost duties will be to carry out any orders that may be required of them by the Military Authorities, and to co-operate with Emergency Committees, who would themselves operate under the same authority.

It is to be borne in mind that the Volunteer Training Corps are being raised for the defence of their Country—and that such measures of defence as may be necessary can only be carried out in conjunction with, and absolutely under the control of, the Military Authorities.

Amongst others the following may be taken as some of the duties which Volunteer Training Corps may with advantage be asked to undertake :—

(a) Assisting in repelling an invasion or raid.

(b) Garrison duties in towns and villages.

(c) Guarding railways and other vulnerable points.

(d) Supervising removal of the civil population, keeping order and allaying panic in case of emergency.

(e) Guarding communications, etc.

The following gives a somewhat more definite statement of the duty of Corps in case of invasion :—

Troops to repel a raid should be in a state of preparation and well aware of the general nature of the service that is required of them. It is obvious that on the first landing of an enemy, if his attempt cannot be frustrated, not a moment should be lost in assembling troops and attacking him with the most advanced, however few in number, till more can be assembled.

The object will be to constantly harass, annoy, and tire out the enemy, and to impede his progress, till a sufficient force can be assembled to smash him. Our Corps must be trained to assist in this, under orders of the proper military authority.

The close nature of our country affords every advantage for offensive action. Intricate and enclosed, it would be exceedingly difficult for an enemy to advance. From his landing he should never be lost sight of, and every inch of ground should be disputed. The Corps should have a good knowledge of the country. Orders have been issued that the country be driven, and cattle and horses removed and everything within reach of the enemy destroyed without mercy. It is here our Corps can offer valuable aid to the Special Constables and Regular Army. If this be carried out efficiently, the future movements of an enemy would become extremely difficult.

It must never be forgotten to inculcate into our Volunteer Corps the great advantages they possess by their knowledge of the country in attacking the enemy.

Active individuals and small Corps may remain in an enclosed country, mostly not suitable for cavalry, within the closest distance of such enemy, watching every opportunity to annoy him.

Every man should be made to understand that, even if worsted in action and forced to retire, his duty requires him to halt and rally and attack again as soon as possible; that he need never hurry, and that he is perfectly safe at a short distance from the enemy.

Above all, it must be impressed upon him that although retiring gradually before the enemy may be at first necessary to allow the Regular troops to collect, yet the great object of irregular Corps is to attack on every favourable opportunity, and as much by the bayonet as by fire; and such attack must be bold and vigorous as becomes men defending their hearths and homes.

There cannot be too many Volunteer Battalions; they are essential for the defence of the country as supports to the Regular Army; and when intelligent and well led and with local knowledge, they will, by their spirit and perseverance, soon attain an ascendancy over the enemy. In this way Volunteer Corps can distinguish themselves in a most honourable manner, and one wholly advantageous to their country.

They must therefore be prepared to move in the lightest manner without baggage of any kind; they must live in temporary shelters, and for this the country is amply suitable. Corps should, having this in view, provide themselves with entrenching tools and bill-hooks for cutting wood. They should carry small kettles; from the rear they will be certain of supplies.

Against our enemy we must employ his own methods, and treat him as he does others; we must raise the indignation of the country to the highest pitch, and cause to re-act on him that terror which he has used in Belgium. In this manner we will successfully oppose him and show him that a free people fighting for the land they love are not to be invaded with impunity.

This is only an outline to let Corps know on what lines they should train, and in anticipation of orders of which we have yet no knowledge. These will come to us definitely in due course from Generals Commanding, who are thoroughly acquainted with local conditions, and for these orders we must wait, but we must be ready for them when they come. And to this end Corps must be well trained, capable of digging up roads, assisting the civil population to move, should be extremely mobile, able to entrench and hut themselves, good shots and with a complete knowledge of all military features of the country of which they are inhabitants. They should have trained scouts able to give all information required to Regular military officers, and to act as guides to troops when necessary.

DUTIES OF COMMANDANTS.

C A.V.T.C.,
30/3/15. **126.** It is highly desirable to keep up the interest of the Units of the Volunteer Training Corps after they have made themselves efficient in elementary drill, entrenching and other duties and until they are supplied with arms and ammunition to practise on open ranges, Commandants therefore should take their men out and study with them the ground in their locality, so that they may acquire a thorough knowledge of, and be in a position to defend the same, or to give information regarding its roads and tracks to any Body of Regular Troops that may be sent into their district for that purpose, and who might require information as to the locality.

The points to which the Commandant should draw the attention of his men would be the vulnerable points in his command and how to defend them, such as :—

> Railway Lines,
> Embankments,
> Cuttings,
> Tunnels,
> Railway Stations,
> Bridges, Roads and Footpaths,
> Telegraph and Telephone Lines and their Stations,
> Rivers and Canals,
> Woods,
> Gas and Electric Light Works,
> Water Supply Reservoirs and Waterworks,
> High Ground, and how to defend it,
> Likely positions for Guns,
> Towns and Villages,

and in Towns and Villages knowledge of :—

> Streets and nearest routes,

Street fighting and Barricades,
Patrol, Picquets, Sentries,
Signalling day and night,
Rapid assembly in case of sudden alarm,
Alarm posts,
Stretcher bearers,
First Aid.

Also where entrenching tools and gangs of labourers are to be found. In fact, all points that would be useful to a Military Force acting in the neighbourhood.

Commandants should also endeavour to organise a system for communicating by bicycle, motor-car or by signalling. Arrangements are being made to organise motor-cars throughout England on a large scale for this purpose, but until this is done local arrangements would be useful.

Should the Commandant have had no previous Military training he could probably be assisted by Members of his unit who have been in the Service.

Plans for the defence of particular posts or localities might be written out as an instruction by those whose military knowledge is equal to it.

Commandants and others requiring horses for mounted duties are reminded that local remount Officers would probably be glad to have Government horses exercised and trained with Volunteer Corps.

DUTIES OF GUIDES.

127. It is extremely important that Members of Volunteer Training Corps should be able to act as Guides, and to do this work efficiently, practice is necessary.

C.A.V.T.C.,
3/8/15,
XL.

As celerity is essential for Guides, and they must be independent of Railways, they should be provided with either a motor, a cycle, or a horse. They should study

F

topography of a given area, which should be roughly two square miles, but the size of the area must depend on the nature of the country.

They should make themselves acquainted with all Railways, including station sidings, approach roads, from rear and front; all roads—including cross roads, bridle paths and footpaths — water supply and available camping grounds; also all lines of telegraph and telephones—aerial and underground; in the country, private houses, &c., in which there are telephones and Post Offices where telegraph or telephones are installed; names of farms and farmers, smiths and forges, wheelwrights, carpenters, and any place where there are stores of entrenching tools, sleepers, timber, wire, or corrugated iron, which might be available. If there is any electric or water supply (light or power) within the area, they should ascertain the course of the mains, and whether they are in the hands of a Company, or Local Authority, with the address of the responsible Manager.

A small note-book of the area should be compiled with references to a six-inch map, giving the above information, or any other which might be useful.

Guides should recollect that all information collected by them might be equally useful to an enemy, so that they must be always ready to destroy it at once by burning, &c., and the Officer to whom they make their report will, if necessary, destroy it, or hand it over to the Staff Officers of the Regular Army under whom he may be acting.

QUALIFICATIONS OF A PLATOON COMMANDER.

128. 1. The Commander of a Platoon must have a clear idea of what is required of a Platoon from the point of view of the Commander of a Company, and understand the interior working of a Platoon.

2. He must know what is required of the soldier as an individual, and when acting with other men.

3. He must have a general knowledge of a Battalion, some idea of what the other arms of the service are, and their general duties.

4. He must be conversant with the following as applied to the training of recruits : —

Elements of Physical Training.—Definitions; Squad drill with and without arms; Section, Platoon and Company drill; Extended Order drill; Training in marching; Guards and Sentries; Entrenching; Outposts; Field work and instructions in night operations; Musketry.

The following books should be consulted : —

Field Service Regulations, Part i., Regulations for the Officers Training Corps, 1912, pages 41, 42, for infantry—for " Section " read " Platoon " ; *Re* Chapter V., Sections 64, 75 to 89; Chapter VII. generally. Manual of Physical Training. Infantry Training, 1914. Musketry Regulations, Part i., Chapter II., Section 4; Chapter III., omitting Sections 17, 23, 24, 29, 32-35. Chapter IV., omitting Sections 45, 54, 56, 62, 63, 64; Chapter V., omitting Sections 70, 71. Manual of Field Engineering.

VOLUNTEER OFFICERS' INSTRUCTIONAL CLASSES.

129. The Central Association has instituted series of Instructional Classes, open to Officers of Volunteer Training Corps and to specially recommended N.C.O.'s and men, with the object of giving them an opportunity of obtaining, under skilful guidance, courses of instruction in Military Subjects which will fit them to carry out their duties in an efficient manner.

The Central Association have decided that before the appointment of an Officer in a Volunteer Training Corps can be officially approved, he must be able to show reasonable efficiency in tactics and interior economy.

The future success of the Volunteers depends on their having efficient officers. On their absolute fitness depends, in a very large measure, the allegiance and ability of the men under their charge; they are answerable for that correct spirit of discipline on which the whole structure of all efficient armed forces rests, and it behoves each one of them to attain such a knowledge of their duties as will command respect and confidence.

Volunteer Officers without previous military training should go through a proper course of instruction. Candidates attending the classes arranged for by the Central Association, and passing the examinations, are recognised as having qualified for appointment as officers.

The object of the examinations is to ascertain if an officer, N.C.O., or man is, or is not, fit practically for promotion to higher rank. The aim is to acquire a personal acquaintance with each candidate, and to test his ability to apply his knowledge practically.

Again, qualified instructors are very difficult to obtain, especially in country districts, and it is hoped that a number of suitable instructors may be developed from these Classes, who will be capable of carrying on the knowledge gained to their respective Corps.

Commandants are adjured to make every endeavour to get their Officers and men to go through these Instructional Classes.

Classes.—The work is at present divided into two classes, as follows:—

> Class A.—A course of Military Lectures, as set forth in the Syllabus below. This course lasts three weeks; and students are examined and Certificates for proficiency are awarded.
> Candidates for this class must be certified as efficient in Drill by the Corps Commanders submitting their names.

Class B.—A course in Drill, as set forth in the
Syllabus below. This course lasts three weeks,
and includes Drill and minor tactical instructions. Certificates for proficiency are awarded.

Candidates.—The names of the candidates, together
with a recommendation (and Certificate in the case of
those attending Class A) from their Commanding
Officers must be submitted to the Central Association of
Volunteer Training Corps by an appointed day.

The Certificate to state that Officers joining Class A
direct are acquainted with the curriculum of Class B,
and are in every way qualified for the position of Officers
in Volunteer Training Corps. Candidates who have
already passed through Class B are eligible for Class A.

The number of members in each Class will be limited,
and nominations are made so as to distribute the selection of candidates accepted among as many Units as
possible.

Fees.—The fee for Classes A and B is fixed at one
and a half guineas for each Class.

Class A, a course of Military Lectures, is one of the
greatest importance to Officers of Volunteer Corps, and
all those who feel they have acquired sufficient knowledge of drill should certainly avail themselves of this
opportunity of gaining knowledge of the more technical,
but not less essential, side of the military duties they will
be expected to perform if their services are to reach the
required standard. The opportunities for the Volunteers
to obtain tuition in the more advanced branches of the
soldier's art are few, and the Central Association con-
fidently rely on all those who can possibly spare the time
to take advantage of the chance presented to them in
Class A of the Instructional Classes.

Circulars are issued from time to time as the dates of
the Classes are arranged, and all those who desire information should communicate with the Secretary,
Volunteer Officers' Instructional Classes, Central Association, who will send full particulars of each course
when ready.

Rules.

1. The wearing of uniform is optional.

2. During drill or lectures no member may address or question the Instructors or any other member. Strict silence must be maintained.

3. Military discipline must be strictly adhered to, both in the letter and spirit.

4. Members are expected to attend punctually and to remain for the whole period of each lecture or drill. Leaving before time seriously disorganises the work, and can be permitted only under exceptional circumstances.

5. The decision of the Central Association must be accepted as final in all cases.

Volunteer Officers' Instructional Classes.
Class A.
Syllabus of Military Lectures.
Three Weeks' Course for Officers.
First Week.

Monday.—	1st hour	Discipline—the soldierly spirit, etc.
	2nd hour	Military Law and King's Regulations.
	3rd hour	Continued.
Tuesday.—	1st hour	Organisation.
	2nd hour	Marching, Theory of.
	3rd hour	March Formations and March Discipline.
Wednesday.—	1st hour	Sanitation in Camps. How to keep fit, etc.
	2nd hour	Drill, Theory of.
	3rd hour	Movements in Extended Order.
Thursday.—	1st hour	Musketry, Theory of.
	2nd hour	Musketry. Fire Positions and Fire Control.
	3rd hour	Duties of Company, Platoon, and Section Commanders.

First Week—*continued.*

Friday.—	1st hour	Entrenchments.
	2nd hour	Notes on Field Engineering, Knotting and Lashing Spars, etc.
	3rd hour	Map Reading.
Saturday.—	1st hour	Map Reading.
	2nd hour	Map Reading.
	3rd hour	Entrenchments.

Second Week.

Monday.—	1st hour	Reconnaissance and Reports.
	2nd hour	Continued.
	3rd hour	Intercommunication and Orders.
Tuesday.—	1st hour	Protection, Advanced and Rear Guards, and Outposts.
	2nd hour	Continued.
	3rd hour	Continued.
Wednesday.—	1st hour	Troops in Battle. The *rôle* of the different arms.
	2nd hour	Artillery in Battle. Theory of use.
	3rd hour	Infantry in Battle. The Attack.
Thursday.—	1st hour	Infantry in Battle. The Defence.
	2nd hour	Entrenchments as made at the Front.
	3rd hour	Clearances and Demolitions.
Friday.—	1st hour	The use of Cover.
	2nd hour	Attack and Defence of Posts.
	3rd hour	Map Reading, etc.
Saturday.—	1st hour	Map Reading and Field Sketching out of doors.
	2nd hour	Continued.
	3rd hour	Continued.

Third Week.

Monday.—   1st hour   Framing of operation Orders.

2nd hour   Field Signals and Messages.

3rd hour   Hints on learning Semaphore, etc.

Tuesday.—   1st hour   Night Operations.

2nd hour   The Company in Attack. Ammunition Supply.

3rd hour   Camps and Bivouacs.

Wednesday.—1st hour   Ceremonial. Customs of the Service.

2nd hour   Guards and Sentries.

3rd hour   General Résumé.

Thursday.—   1st hour
2nd hour }Prepare for Examination.
3rd hour

Friday.—   1st hour
2nd hour }Examination.
3rd hour

Saturday.—   1st hour
2nd hour }Examination.
3rd hour

VOLUNTEER OFFICERS' INSTRUCTIONAL CLASSES.

CLASS B.

SYLLABUS OF OFFICERS' DRILL COURSE.

First Week.

Monday.—   1st hour   Open Section Drill.

2nd hour   Instructions in Words of Command.

Tuesday.—   1st hour   Two Rank Drill.

2nd hour   Instructions in Words of Command.

Wednesday.—   No Drill.

Thursday.—   1st hour   Bayonet Fighting.

2nd hour   Two Rank Drill — Officers in turn.

First Week —*continued.*

Friday.— 1st hour Arm Drill.
            2nd hour Care of Arms and Parts of Rifle.
Saturday.— 1st hour Musketry.
            2nd hour Squad Drill with Arms.

Second Week.

Monday.— 1st hour Squad Drill with Arms.
            2nd hour Extended Order Drill.
Tuesday.— 1st hour Company and Battalion Drill (lecture).
            2nd hour Platoon Drill.
Wednesday.— No Drill.
Thursday.— 1st hour Bayonet Fighting.
            2nd hour Company Drill.
Friday.— 1st hour Company Drill (continued).
            2nd hour Company Drill, Officers in turn.
Saturday.— 1st hour Company Drill, Officers in turn (continued).
            2nd hour Company Drill, Officers in turn (continued).

Third Week.

Monday.— 1st hour Battalion Drill (lecture).
            2nd hour Company in the Attack.
Tuesday.— 1st hour Platoon and Section in Extended Order.
            2nd hour Company Drill. Officers to give off Detail.
Wednesday.— No Drill.
Thursday.— 1st hour Instructions in Fire Orders and Outposts.
            2nd hour Company Drill to test Officers.
Friday.— 1st hour Guards and Sentries.
            2nd hour Questioning Officers about Drill.
Saturday.— 1st hour Sword Drill.
            2nd hour Wind up.

HOME STUDY COURSE.

ORGANISATION.

(H.S. 1.) **129a.** The Central Association is prepared to issue an Official Examination Certificate to those Officers and N.C.O.'s who have undertaken a course of home study on the approved lines laid down in C.A. Form H.S.2, and who successfully pass examinations to be held in their respective Counties from time to time as may be arranged. A circular (H.S.1) detailing the organisation and procedure of Examining Boards will be supplied to Commandants on application.

GENERAL DIRECTIONS AND SYLLABUS OF STUDY.

(H.S. 2.) *Object.*—It is recognised that a great many officers and N.C.O.'s of Volunteer Training Corps are willing to prepare themselves for examination in military subjects, by undertaking a course of Home Study, or by attending local training classes. Having this in view the Central Association have decided to make the necessary arrangements, through the County Organisations, for examinations to be held in various centres at stated intervals (see Form H.S.1).

Examining Board.—A Board will be appointed in each County where a County Organisation exists, to superintend each examination held, in accordance with the directions given in Form H.S.1.

Registration.—All officers (below the rank of Company Commander) and N.C.O.'s who desire to attend such examinations should approach their Company Commander on the subject, notifying him that they intend taking up home study; he will then register their names as prospective candidates. They will be informed as to what arrangements are being made in the matter, and in due course will make application to attend for examination in the manner prescribed below. Officers of and above the rank of Company Commander will make application to attend for examination in the manner hereinafter laid down in paragraph 3 of " Rules Governing the Application for Examination."

Eligibility.—All officers and N.C.O.'s of Volunteer Training Corps duly affiliated to the Central Association are eligible for examination, always provided they can obtain the necessary certificate from their superior officer, and are acceptable to the Examining Board. All those making application must have a good knowledge of Company Drill; this is essential.

Rules and Regulations.—Rules and Regulations governing the application for examination are given below. Prospective candidates must also make themselves familiar with the contents of Form H.S.1.

Scope of Examination.—Candidates will be examined in any or all of the following subjects : —

> Military Law and King's Regulations.
> Organisation.
> Infantry Training.
> Musketry.
> Map Reading and Field Sketching.
> Reconnaissance.
> Field Engineering.
> Elementary Military Hygiene.

and will be expected to have a good general knowledge of the contents of the official handbooks on these subjects. The examinations will be entirely written; and to pass, a candidate must obtain .5 in each of the subjects. Special certificates will be granted to those candidates who receive .75 or over in each subject.

Previous Military or other Training.—Those with previous military training can enter for examination direct, *i.e.*, without going through a course of home study, provided that they can satisfy their Company Commander or Battalion Commandant that they are in every way qualified to take full advantage of the examination. This also applies to those who have attended the Instructional Classes organised by the Central Association, or local instructional classes duly recognised by the Central Association. A candidate who has put in a full attendance at such a class shall be deemed as eligible for examination.

Fees.—Each candidate, as and when he makes application for permission to attend for examination, will pay an Examination Fee of half-a-guinea. Such fees will be forwarded, with applications, to the Examining Board, who will, if any application be refused, cause the Examination Fee to be refunded.

Places and Times.—The Examining Board appointed in each County will arrange, through the County Executive Committee, for examinations to be held at places and times most convenient to the majority, on the dates set from time to time by the Central Association. Due notice of arrangements must be given to all Corps concerned.

Correspondence.—All correspondence should be submitted through the proper channel (see paragraph 75, Official Regulations). Candidates, or prospective candidates, for examination must on no account write direct to the Central Association on any matter arising out of these Home Study Courses.

Syllabus of Course of Home Study.

The papers will be set to test the candidate's ability in applying his knowledge of the subject matter contained in:—

Manual of Military Law. Chapters I., II., IX., XI., XIV. (2s.)

The Army Act. General Idea of Contents.

King's Regulations. General Idea of Contents and Paras. 1-13, 1765-1804, 1841-1864. (1s.)

Field Service Regulations, Part I. Chapters I., II., III., Sections 24 to 33 inclusive; Chapters V., VII., IX. (6d.)

Infantry Training. Definitions, and Chapters I., V., VIII., IX., X., XI., XIV. (6d.)

Musketry Regulations, Part I. Chapters I., II., Section 9 to 14, III., IV., V., Section 17. (6d.)

Manual of Map Reading. Chapters I., II., III., IV., V., VI., VII., XII. (1s.)

Notes on Map Reading for Use in Army Schools. All. (3d.)

Manual of Field Engineering. Definitions— Chapters I., II., III., IV., V., VI., IX., X., XIV., XV. (9d.)

Manual of Elementary Military Hygiene. Chapters I., V., VI., VIII., X. (6d.)

and their home studies must be guided by this syllabus.

Candidates can supplement their studies of the Official Handbooks by reference to the following books:—

Tactical Talks and Tramps. By "Sextus." (Specially recommended.) Copies can be obtained from the Central Association, post free 1s. 8d. Published by Baily and Woods.

Drill and Field Training; Ceremonial; Field Entrenchments; Musketry. Imperial Army Series. Published by John Murray, London. (1s. each.)

Military Sketching and Map Reading for N.C.O.'s and men. By Major R. F. Legge. Published by Gale and Polden. (1s, 6d.)

Company Drill; Battalion Drill. Capt. C. C. Esson. Published by Harrison & Sons. (6d. and 1s. each respectively.)

The following books are useful as containing questions and answers:—

Hythe Musketry Course made Easy; Notes on Visual Training and Judging Distance. By 2nd Lieut. J. Bostock. Published by Gale and Polden. (1s. and 6d. each respectively.)

NOTE.—The figures placed in brackets denote the prices of books, exclusive of postal charges.

RULES GOVERNING THE APPLICATION FOR EXAMINATION.

1. Candidates must be officers or N.C.O.'s of Volunteer Training Corps affiliated to the Central Association Volunteer Training Corps. Officers and N.C.O.'s shall be eligible for examination provided they receive the necessary recommendation from their Superior Officer.

2. Candidates below the rank of Company Commander must make application for permission to attend for examination, through their Company Commanders, at least four weeks in advance of date set for such examination, on C.A. Form H.S.3.

A Company Commander or Sub-Commandant of a Battalion desirous of becoming a candidate for examination will fill in C.A. Form H.S.3, and forward it to his Battalion Commandant, who will, if he thinks proper, forward the form to the Examining Board concerned, together with a recommendation on C.A. Form H.S.4.

A Commandant of a Battalion desirous of becoming a candidate for examination will fill in C.A. Form H.S.3, and forward it to the Board appointed to superintend examinations in his County, for their approval.

3. Company Commanders shall forward applications received by them to their Battalion Commandants,

together with certificates of recommendation (on C.A. Form H.S.4). A Company Commander before recommending an officer or N.C.O. as suitable for examination should satisfy himself that each applicant is qualified to attend and take full advantage of the examination.

4. Battalion Commandants shall forward the application forms and certificates of suitable candidates to the Board appointed to superintend Examinations in their respective Counties, who shall, when an application has been accepted, issue to the Battalion Commandant concerned a card (C.A. Form H.S.5), stating that applicant must present himself for examination at an appointed place and hour. When these cards reach the hands of Battalion Commandants they shall immediately cause them to be forwarded to the O.C. the unit concerned, who shall at once cause them to be issued to the candidates, together with copies of any circulars dealing with the examination. It is imperative this be done without delay.

5. Candidates must conform in every respect with such rules and regulations as may be issued by the Central Association from time to time governing these examinations. Care should be taken that each candidate is fully conversant with such rules and regulations.

6. Each candidate shall pay the sum of half-a-guinea to the Central Association as entrance fee for examination, such sum to be payable through the Board appointed to superintend examinations in applicant's County.

7. The decision of the Central Association must be accepted as final in all cases.

SIGNALLING CLASSES.

129b. The Central Association of Volunteer Training Corps has instituted a series of Instructional Classes open to members of Volunteer Training Corps, with the object of giving them an opportunity of obtaining, under skilful guidance, courses of instruction in the various branches of Army Signalling, viz., Flag Signalling (Morse and Semaphore), Discs, and Lamps, and the combined Buzzer and Field Telephone.

The Central Association views it as a matter of prime importance that field operations in signalling by Volunteer Training Corps should be carried out on strict military lines, so that Corps may work with a complete understanding. With this end in view Commandants of Volunteer Training Corps are urged to encourage their men to attend these Classes for standardised instruction, and to utilise the services of the Central Association Instructors, by arranging for their signallers to attend these Classes and to be examined for proficiency, and the right to wear the signalling badge issued by the Central Association.

The object of the examination is to ascertain if an Officer, N.C.O., or man is, or is not, qualified to wear the Central Association's Badge. The aim is to acquire a personal acquaintance with each candidate, and to test his ability to apply his knowledge practically and theoretically.

Class.—The work of the Class will be divided into two Sections, as follows:—

Section A.—A course of technical lectures explanatory of the Theory and Construction of the signalling instruments, *i.e.*, Lamps, Buzzer and Field Telephones, including the method of connecting up the stations by wires and cable and the electrical connections at the Signalling Stations, *and practical work in connection therewith.*

Section B.—A course of lectures explanatory of the requirements in connection with all branches of Signalling duties, *and practical work in connection therewith.*

One hour each evening will be devoted to lectures and one hour to practical work in connection with each Section with the various apparatus and plant. Lectures and practical work under Sections A and B will be taken on alternate days. Practical work in the field will also be arranged for on Saturdays, as opportunity arises. *Officers, N.C.O.'s, and men are eligible to enter the class.*

Fees.—The fee for the class is half-a-guinea. All fees are payable in advance, and should be forwarded with application. Fees sent in by those whose applications are not accepted will be returned as soon as practicable after the closing date for entry.

Books.—The undermentioned books are recommended :—

Army Training Manual, Signalling, Parts I. and II

Imperial Army Series, " Signalling " (published by John Murray).

Syllabus of Lectures.

Section A.

1. Elementary principles of Magnetism and Electricity.
2. Theory and construction of Lamps, Buzzers and Vibrators.
3. The application of the principles of Magnetism and Electricity to Telephony.
4. The theory and construction of Telephone Transmitters and Receivers.
5. The construction of lines, method of making connections and wire joints.
6. Laying of telephone cable in the open or in the trenches.

G

7. Methods to be adopted to avoid interference from neighbouring circuits.
8. Detection of interference with the lines by hostile forces.
9. Instrument and Line faults.
10. Construction of Batteries, Testing and Maintenance.

Section B.

1. Moving and Fixed Stations.
2. Selection of positions for Stations.
3. Methods of communication.
4. Backgrounds, Skylines, Concealment.
5. Allocation and duties of Signallers at stations.
6. Duties of Signal Officers.
7. Procedure in connection with message forms, including counting of words, meaning of special symbols, method of writing.
8. The signalling and repetition of figures.
9. Cypher Groups, Codes, and prefixes.
10. General principles of communication work.

Examination.—At the conclusion of the course candidates will be examined, by the Instructors, in the subjects comprising the Course. The qualifying badge for signalling, authorised by the Central Association, will be awarded, together with a special certificate for proficiency, to those passing the examination. The qualifying standards for the Signalling Badge are given in paragraph 111.

RULES.

1. The wearing of uniform is optional.

2.—Members must provide themselves with two standard flags, 2 ft. by 2 ft., with 3 ft. 6 in. pole. Lamps, Buzzer and Telephone Instruments will, as far as possible, be provided by the Central Association.

3. Members are expected to attend punctually and to remain for the whole period of each lecture or drill. Leaving before time seriously disorganises the work, and can be permitted only under exceptional circumstances.

4. The decision of the Central Association must be accepted as final in all cases.

5. During drill or lectures no member may address or question the Instructors or any other member. Strict silence must be maintained.

6. Military discipline must be strictly adhered to, both in the letter and spirit.

Full particulars of above can be obtained on application to The Secretary, Volunteer Officers' Instructional Classes, C.A.V.T.C.

THE HAGUE CONVENTION.

130. The legality of the Volunteer Movement is set out in the following quotation from the Hague Convention : —

SECTION I.—OF BELLIGERENTS.

CHAPTER I.—THE STATUS OF BELLIGERENT.

Article I.—The laws, rights, and duties of war apply not only to the Army, but also to Militia and Volunteer Corps fulfilling all the following conditions : —

1. They must be commanded by a person responsible for his subordinates;
2. They must have a fixed distinctive sign recognisable at a distance;
3. They must carry arms openly; and
4. They must conduct their operations in accordance with the laws and customs of war.

In countries where Militia or Volunteer Corps constitute the Army, or form part of it, they are included under the denomination "Army."

That Corps affiliated to this Central Association are included under the denomination " Army " is borne out by the three Official Recognitions by the State of the Volunteer Corps affiliated to this Association.

1. Statement by the Prime Minister in the House of Commons on the 17th November, 1914, in reply to a question by Sir Henry Craik; which stated that the Government had decided to recognise the C.A.V.T.C. and Corps affiliated thereto (see para. 2).

2. Letter signed by Sir R. Brade on behalf of the Army Council addressed to Lord Desborough as President of the Central Association Volunteer Training Corps, dated the 19th November, 1914, confirming this recognition, and stating the conditions of recognition (see para. 7).

3. Statement by the Home Office to the Lord Lieutenants of certain counties in the United Kingdom, dated 30/11/14 (see para. 13).

The conditions laid down by Rule 1 of Article I. of the Hague Convention are met by the War Office Regulations and Rules of the Central Association. Only Corps are recognised by the Association that can satisfy their Inspecting Officers that they are being properly conducted and commanded by competent Officers.

Rule 2 of Article I. is met by the 5-inch Brassard, which is red, and when fixed is a " distinctive sign recognisable at a distance."

Rules 3 and 4 naturally would be adhered to because, in case of invasion, Corps would come under the control of the General Officer in command of the District.

VOLUNTEER TRAINING CORPS FIELD AMBULANCE.

RULES AND REGULATIONS.

130a. 1. The rules and regulations of the Central Association and the War Office for the conduct of Volunteer Training Corps, in so far as they are applicable to V.T.C. Field Ambulance, shall be adhered to.

2. The training of such Corps shall be on the lines laid down in " Royal Army Medical Corps Training, 1911." A syllabus of training will be found on pages 10/11.

3. The portions of Infantry Training to be used in a V.T.C. Field Ambulance are those dealing with : —

> Definitions.
>
> Squad Drill (without arms).
>
> Company Drill (without arms).

See Part IV., " Royal Army Medical Corps Training, 1911."

4. The personnel for a Field Ambulance Section attached to a Battalion V.T.C. shall be as below, and shall be known as a V.T.C. Field Ambulance Section. Nor must this establishment be exceeded for each Battalion.

> Medical Officer Commanding, with rank of Company Commander, 1.
>
> Medical Officers, ranking as Platoon Commanders, 2.
>
> Quartermaster, ranking as Platoon Commander, 1.
>
> Warrant Officer with rank of Battalion Sergeant-Major, 1.
>
> Staff Sergeant, with rank of Company Sergeant-Major, 1.

Sergeants, ranking as Section Commanders, 2.

Rank and File qualified on the lines laid down in "Royal Army Medical Corps Training, 1911," 25.

Bugler, 1.

Making a minimum total of 34.

To make up complete establishments there should be thirty more trained men, but if these are not available, men can be detailed to act as bearers from the Infantry Battalion, 30.

Total, 64.

Apart from and in addition to this Field Ambulance each Battalion should have 16 men trained as Stretcher Bearers who will not form part of the Ambulance personnel.

5. All such Detachments in a County shall be linked up, and three such Sections shall be known as V.T.C. Field Ambulance, and be available when the County Volunteers are working as a Regiment.

6. A County Medical Commandant, with V.T.C. rank of Battalion Commandant, shall be appointed by the County President on the advice of the Regimental Commandant, and he shall be responsible for the organisation, training and inspection of the V.T.C. Field Ambulance throughout the County.

7. The appointment of all Officers to V.T.C. Ambulance shall be by the County President, acting on the advice of the County Medical Commandant, and on the lines laid down in Official Regulations of V.T.C. for the appointment of Officers.

8. No Officer shall be appointed except he has a recognised Medical qualification, with the exception of the Quartermaster.

9. Members of V.T.C. Field Ambulance must wear, when in uniform, the Official Ambulance Badge of the

Central Association. If they are embodied as a Field Ambulance for Active Service, they would be supplied, when they are called out, with the Government Red Cross Armlet. Until such eventuality the red cross cannot be worn, but the official ambulance badge of the Central Association should be worn on the right sleeve. See para. 114.

10. All men must qualify for the Field Ambulance by obtaining the First Aid Certificate of the British Red Cross Society and the St. John's Ambulance Association.

11. An Officer in Command of the Field Ambulance Section must keep a record of all Classes of Instruction in technical subjects as regards dates, number attended, and progress. He will be responsible that every N.C.O. and men serving under his Command is afforded facilities to attend all classes that may be necessary to qualify for advancement, and he will inquire into the causes of all instances of N.C.O.'s and men, who, being eligible to qualify, do not attend the prescribed courses. After they have obtained the First Aid Certificate they should be trained in Field work as Stretcher Bearers, in nursing duties, in clerk's duties, cook's duties and transport duties, but the general training of the men for their duties must be carried out by the Sectional Medical Officers supervised by the County Medical Commandant.

SECTION V.

———

SECTION V.

NATIONAL MOTOR VOLUNTEERS.

(Not applicable to motors registered by the Government.)

131. The Rules and Regulations of the Central Association Volunteer Training Corps as regards uniform, badges of rank, and discipline shall be strictly adhered to, with the exceptions hereinafter laid down. C.A.V.T.C., Rules to be adhered to.

132. A separate Section of the Central Association of Volunteer Training Corps has been established at the Association Headquarters, Judges' Quadrangle, Royal Courts of Justice, to which is entrusted, under the general direction of the Executive Committee, the duty of dealing with all questions relating to the National Motor Volunteers. The Officer in charge of this Section and Commandant, should the Units be required for National purposes, is Major-General D. C. F. Macintyre, C.B. He will work in communication with the Executive Military Department, and is a member of the Military Committee of the Central Association. Officer in Charge.

Objects of National Motor Volunteers.

133. 1. To assist recruiting for the Regular and Territorial Army. Objects of the National Motor Volunteers.

2. To encourage Motorists and Motor Cyclists disqualified for service in the Regular Forces.

> (a) To form themselves into Motor Volunteer Corps so as to be available for Military duties.

(b) To teach members of such Corps the elements of drill and rifle shooting.

N.B.—If of military age they must agree in writing to enlist if called upon to do so as per War Office Letter 20/Gen.No./3604 (A.G.1.) of the 19th November, 1914.

3. To organise such Motor Corps into County or City Regimental Organisations, which, while preserving their autonomy in the same way as Volunteer Training Corps Battalions of County Regiments, will be under the Command of the Commandant of the County Volunteer Regiments. To see that the rules of the Army Council conditional to the recognition of Volunteers are strictly adhered to, both in the letter and spirit.

N.B.—In cases where Motorists, Motor Cyclists or Cyclists are at present attached to Volunteer Battalions nothing in this rule shall be held to require their detachment therefrom.

Duties of National Motor or Cycle Volunteers.

Duties of National Motor or Cycle Volunteers are:—

134. 1. When attached to Battalions to act as scouts, carry reinforcements, or act as Battalion transport.

2. In cases where they have an organisation apart from Battalions—

In communication with County Commandants or with the property constituted Military Authorities—the rapid conveyance of troops to any threatened point, in the case of an invasion or raid or other case of military necessity. Should time permit these military duties will always be carried out with the previous sanction of the County or City Regimental Commandant. Should time not permit of this, a report must invariably be made to the County or City Regimental Commandant as soon as possible of the military duty done, and an explanation given of why his previous orders were not obtained.

3. Scouting, intelligence work, if undertaken at the request of the Military Authorities, must be reported to the County or City Regimental Commandant, and previous sanction obtained should time permit.

4. Hospital work, such as conveyance of wounded and health rides to convalescent soldiers and sailors. For this the previous sanction of the County Commandant is not necessary, but he will, should he so desire, be kept acquainted with what is done.

5. Conveyance of arms, munitions and food for troops or Volunteers, if undertaken at request of military authorities, is to be reported to County or City Regimental Commandant, and previous sanction obtained should time permit.

135. The bases of organisation shall be the County. Organisation The Unit shall be the Squadron. Where there are a sufficient number of Squadrons they may, with the sanction of the County or City Commandant, be organised into Battalions. Such Squadrons or Battalions shall work with and under the command of County or City Commandants, and while part of the County Organisation, shall remain distin t from the Infantry and Engineer Volunteers in the same way as such do in the Regular Army. They shall be available for National purposes as well as for those of their County. Rules for the national duties on which they may be required will be issued as soon as the Organisation develops.

N.B.—Nothing in this rule shall be held to interfere with the status of those motor or motor cyclists or bicycle Volunteers which are at present an integral part of Battalions.

RULES.

136. 1. Those eligible for service in Motor Volunteer Membership. Training Corps must be owners or drivers of motor cars or motor cycles (private or commercial), who are not qualified for service in the Regular Forces, and must comply with the terms of the War Office Letter of the 19th November, 1914, reference number 20/Gen.No./ 3604 (A.G.I.). (See Para. 7.)

Officers. 2. A Commandant shall be appointed for each Motor Volunteer Corps on the recommendation of the County Commandant, with the approval and formal appointment of the President of the County Committee of the County Volunteer Training Corps. The nomination of other Officers shall lie with the Commandant of the County Motor Volunteers and on the recommendation of the County Regimental Commandant, subject to the formal appointment of the President of the Committee of the County Volunteer Training Corps.

The Central Association has approved of the ranks of Squadron and Half-Squadron Commander for Officers of the National Motor Volunteers. These ranks will correspond with those of Company and Platoon Commander respectively, and have the same badges of rank.

Register. 3. The Commandant of each Company must keep a Register—

    (a) Of all the vehicles available, with full particulars of the make and horsepower of the cars and motor cycles, seating capacity, registered letters, numbers and type of body.

    (b) Of the days and hours the cars, etc., will be at the disposal of the Section.

Returns. 4. A return must be kept of the public duties each car performs, which must be forwarded monthly to the Commandant of the County Motor Volunteers.

Inspections. 5. Regular periodical inspections must be made of all the squadrons or units forming the County Motor Volunteer Corps by the Commandant of the County or City Regiment, and the reports thereon must be dispatched to and filed at County Headquarters so as to be available whenever required for inspection by the Officer deputed from the C.A.V.T.C. Headquarters for this purpose—who will ordinarily be the Officer in charge of the National Motor Volunteers Section.

137. 6. The special badge designed for the Motor Section must be worn on the cap, and the designation of the Motor unit on the shoulder bands as follows :—

The car badge (as under) must be fixed in a prominent position on the cars or motor cycles of all members.

7. (a) Members of a Motor Volunteer Corps must undergo a course of training in the necessary military duties.

(b) Members must qualify in the elements of drill as laid down in "Infantry Training 1914."

Special *exemption* may be given to a driver of a car or motor cycle by the County Commandant on the recommendation of the Motor Unit Commandant, provided he can show that the proposed driver is disqualified physically from undergoing the necessary training, though able to discharge his duties as a motorist or motor cyclist. These exemptions should be, however, granted very sparingly and only in

the interest of Corps as special cases. It must
be recollected that a driver who cannot
satisfy this military test is of much less value
to a defence force than the ones who can.

(c) Where no special rules are laid down for members
of the Motor Volunteer Section, those applicable to Volunteers generally will be held to
apply to them.

8. The Rules and Regulations of the Central Association Volunteer Training Corps as regards
ranks, uniform, badges and general conduct
of a Volunteer Corps, in so far as they are
applicable to a Motor Corps, shall be strictly
adhered to, and any infringement of same
will make a Corps liable to disaffiliation.

APPENDICES.

APPENDIX 1.

Form XII.

CENTRAL ASSOCIATION VOLUNTEER TRAINING CORPS.

Royal Courts of Justice, W.C.

.... 1915.

CORPS REGISTER.

FORM TO BE FILLED IN ON ENROLMENT.

Corps :—

Headquarters : –

1. Name ....
   Permanent Address ....
   Married or Single ....
   If Married, number of children, age, sex of each ....

2. Age ....
   Height ....
   Chest Measurement ....

3. Reasons for not joining Regular Forces ....
   ....
   ....
   ....

4. Previous Military Training (if any) ....
   ....
   ....

5. Occupation (giving special qualification, *e.g.*, Telegraphist,
   Mechanic, Etc.) ....
   ....
   ....
   ....

6. Whether possessing Horse, Motor-car, Motor-van, Motor-cycle,
   or Bicycle ....

   Signature of Member ....

   Signature of Commandant ....

7. I accept the terms of the War Office Letter to Lord Desborough $\frac{20}{\text{Gen. No.}}$ (A.G.I.), dated 19th November, 1914.
   $\frac{}{3604}$

   Signed ....

To be signed by Recruits of MILITARY AGE.

H

APPENDIX 2.

AFFILIATION FORM.

FORM XIV.   COUNTY EDITION.

(To be filled up for each Company in the Battalions of the County Regiment.)

County ....

Battalion to which Company belongs ....

Name of Company ....
District or Villages from which Men are drawn (see back).

Name and Address of Company Commander ....

....

Headquarters for Communications ....

....

Nearest Railway Station ....

Number of Men in Company—

    (a) Above Military Age ....

    (b) Of Military Age ....

All the latter must sign acceptance of the terms of the War Office letter No. 20/Gen. No./3604, dated 19th November, 1914.

Signature of Regimental Commandant Approving above Company

....

APPENDIX 3.

AFFILIATION FORM.

FORM XIV.   LONDON EDITION.

Commandants are requested to fill up this form for each Company of a Battalion, even when each Company of the Battalion has the same Headquarters.

_____

Regiment ....

Battalion to which Company belongs ....

Name of Company ....

District from which Men are drawn (see back).

Headquarters and Address—

    (a) Battalion ....

....

    (b) Company ....

....

Nearest Railway Station to Company Headquarters ....

Number of Men in Company—

    (a) Above Military Age ....

    (b) Of Military Age ....

All the latter must sign acceptance of the terms of the War Office letter No. 20/Gen. No./3604, dated 19th November, 1914.

Signature of Regimental Commandant approving above Company

....

APPENDIX 4.

MODEL FORM OF APPOINTMENT FOR OFFICERS.

County of London Volunteer Regiments.

To .... of ....

I, Robert, Marquess of Crewe, Lord Lieutenant of the County of London, acting as President of the Grand Council of the County of London Volunteer Training Corps, and acting on the advice of .... Regimental Commandant of the .... London Volunteer Regiment, do hereby approve the appointment of you the said .... to be .... in the .... Volunteer Corps under the command of .... acting as .... thereof.

AND you, the said .... are to observe and follow such orders and directions from time to time as you shall receive from your Regimental Commandant or any other your Superior Officer, according to the rules and customs of War and in pursuance of the trust hereby reposed in you.

SIGNED by me, ... at .... in the County of .... this..................... day of .... in the year of our Lord one thousand nine hundred and fifteen.

APPENDIX 5.

9TH AUGUST, 1915.   XIII. (REVISED EDITION).

CENTRAL ASSOCIATION VOLUNTEER TRAINING CORPS.

INSPECTION REPORT.

1. Name of County Regiment ....

2. Name of Company or Battalion.   (If part of a Battalion name or number of such Battalion) ....
....
....
....

3. (a) Headquarters ....
   (b) Parade Ground, Drill Hall or other place where Unit is trained ....
....
....
....

4. Date and place of inspection ....
....

5. Name and address of Unit Commandant ....
....

6. Officers : Names and efficiency of Company and Platoon Commanders (state if any Officer has had previous Military Training) ....
....
....
....
....

   Adjutant ....
   Signalling Officer ....
   Cyclist Officer ....
   Transport Officer ....
   Medical Officer ....
   Sergeant-Major ....

Other N.C.O's...

....

....

7. Corps Register. State if correctly kept and on C.A. Form...

....

No. of Members (a) from 19 to 40 ....

(b) from 40 to 45 who have served in the
Regular Army, Militia, Special Reserve,
Volunteer or Territorial Forces for not
less than one year ....

(c) Under 19 .... (d) Over 40............

State whether all men of Military Age have signed the
acceptance of the terms of the War Office letter of 19th

November, 1914 $\frac{20\ \text{Gen. No.}}{3604}$ (A.G.I.) ....

....

....

8. Brassards. (a) No. received .... (b) No. still required.........

9. Musketry ....

....

10. Entrenching ....

....

11. No. of Cyclists trained to work together ....

12. Motor Section (if any) and transport ....

....

....

13. Mounted Section ....

....

14. No. and classification of Signallers ....

....

15. Ambulance Section.

(a) No. of men acting as Bearer Detachment ....

(b) No. of Stretchers, First Aid Haversacks, Triangular
Bandages, Splints, etc. ....

....

....

(c) How many men hold certificates of efficiency ....

16. Drill. Standard reached ....,

    ....,

17. Field Training ....

    ....

18. Parade State ....

    ....

19. Uniform. Colour and cloth used, and whether according to
    regulations ....

    ....

20. Band ....

21. Number and make of Rifles, Bayonets and Ammunition.........

    ....

    ....

22. Ranges (a) Full ....
             (b) Miniature ....

23. Name of Armourer ....

24. Is any interest taken in Corps by Civil Authorities..............

    ....

    ....

25. Funds ....

    ....

26. Requirements of Corps ....

    ....

    ....

    ....

27. General Remarks of Inspecting Officer ....

    ....

    ....

    ....

    ....

    Signature of Inspecting Officer ....,.....

APPENDIX 6.

MARCH 30TH, 1915.   FORM XXVII.

SERVICES THAT MEMBERS OF A VOLUNTEER CORPS ARE ABLE TO GIVE.

Please answer fully the undermentioned questions.

1. Are you prepared to do Patrol Work locally at night :—
   - (a) What evenings.
   - (b) At what times.

2. Are you prepared to do Patrol Work locally by day :—
   - (a) What days.
   - (b) At what times.

3. Are you prepared to go away for a week at a time.
   - (a) At what intervals of time.
   - (b) At your own expense.

4. In case of Invasion, in addition to service near your home, would you be prepared to serve in any part of your County.

5. In case of Invasion, in addition to service near your home, would you be prepared to serve in any part of the United Kingdom.

N.B. This offer of service is voluntary. Particulars are required for information only and are not binding. The Authorities, however, have made no alterations in their original letter as to financial assistance.

These forms can be supplied at the rate of 2s. hundred, post free.

APPENDIX 7.

THIRD EDITION. SEPTEMBER, 1915. FORM XI.

REPORT FORM (COUNTY EDITION).

QUARTERLY REPORT OF COMMANDANT
_____ BATTALION _____ COUNTY.

To be sent in duplicate to County Headquarters 1st October, 1st January, 1st April, and 1st July.

Address and Headquarters of Battalion :   Strength of Company.
Do.   do.   No. 1 Company :   1
Do.   do.   No. 2 Company :   2
Do.   do.   No. 3 Company :   3
Do.   do.   No. 4 Company :   4

Number of Men obtained for Regular Army during Quarter :

Number of Men in Battalion :—
  1. Of Military Age
  2. Not of Military Age   } Total _____

Strength of Motor Section.
  Do.   of Cyclist Section.
  Do.   of Signalling Section.
  Do.   of Ambulance Section.

Number of Men willing to :
  1. Do Patrol Work at night locally.
  2.   ,,   ,,   by day   ,,
  3. Go away for a week at a time.
  4. Serve in case of invasion in any part of the County.
  5.   ,,   ,,   ,,   ,,   ,,   United Kingdom.

Equipment :—1. No. of Rifles, Etc.
           2. Ammunition—Rounds of.
           3. Uniforms—No. of Men supplied with.

Service done and on whose authority :
  1. Patrol or Guard Work.
  2. Entrenching.

* Report on Training :—

Signature _____
Battalion Commandant.

Date _____

* State very briefly how many Parades outside the barrack square or other regular drill ground, and their nature, whether Field Days, Route March, Night Operations, &c,

INDEX.

GREAT WAR MEMOIRS, BIOGRAPHIES

Not for nothing has the First World War gone down in history as the most literate, and literary, ever fought. The products of mass education went into action en masse for the first time, and in the case of junior officers, the products of classical education went too. The result was an unprecedented mass of written material from the trenches. This a selection from our published stock that cover both sides of the wire.

MEDAL WITHOUT BAR
An English War Novel
Richard Blaker
9781783314249

1916-1918 A WAR DIARY
By H M Adams MC Worcester Regt.
9781783317271

THE ADVANCE FROM MONS 1914
By Walter Bloem with a Foreword by Sir James E. Edmonds
9781783317523

MY .75
REMINISCENCES OF A GUNNER OF A 75M/M BATTERY
By Paul Lintier
9781783317936

IRON TIMES WITH THE GUARDS
By an "O. E." (Pseudonym of Lt. G. P. A. Fildes, Coldstream Guards)
9781783312924

MERRY HELL! A DANE WITH THE CANADIANS
By Thomas Dinesen, VC
9781845740962

GUN FODDER
A DIARY OF FOUR YEARS OF WAR
by A.Hamilton Gibbs
9781845741686

OLD SOLDIERS NEVER DIE
By Frank Richards, DCM, MM.
9781843420262

LANGEMARCK AND CAMBRAI
By Capt Geoffrey Dugdale
9781845742683

MY WAR MEMORIES 1914-1918
By General Ludendorff
9781845743031

A BRIGADIER IN FRANCE
By Hanway R.Cumming
9781843421320

OVER THE TOP. A "P.B.I." in the H.A.C
By Arthur Lambert
9781843421269

AT G.H.Q.
By Brigadier General John Charteris CMG DSO
9781474538039

www.ingramcontent.com/pod-product-compliance
Lightning Source LLC
Chambersburg PA
CBHW072026040426
42447CB00009B/1748